The WAY *of*
ABUNDANCE

Also by Ann Voskamp

Be the Gift

The Broken Way

The Broken Way Study Guide with DVD

One Thousand Gifts:
A Dare to Live Fully Right Where You Are

One Thousand Gifts Devotional:
Reflections on Finding Everyday Grace

Selections from One Thousand Gifts:
Finding Joy in What Really Matters

One Thousand Gifts Study Guide with DVD

The Greatest Gift:
Unwrapping the Full Love Story of Christmas

Unwrapping the Greatest Gift:
A Family Celebration of Christmas

The Wonder of the Greatest Gift:
An Interactive Family Celebration of Advent

The WAY *of* ABUNDANCE

A 60-DAY JOURNEY INTO A
DEEPLY MEANINGFUL LIFE

ANN VOSKAMP

ZONDERVAN

The Way of Abundance
Copyright © 2018 by Ann Morton Voskamp

Requests for information should be addressed to:
Zondervan, *3900 Sparks Dr. SE, Grand Rapids, Michigan 49546*

ISBN 978-0-310-35267-9 (international trade paper edition)

ISBN 978-0-310-35204-4 (audio)

ISBN 978-0-310-35129-0 (ebook)

Library of Congress Cataloging-in-Publication Data

Names: Voskamp, Ann, 1973- author.
Title: The way of abundance : a 60-day journey into a deeply meaningful life / Ann Voskamp.
Description: Grand Rapids : Zondervan, [2018]
Identifiers: LCCN 2017047623 | ISBN 9780310350316 (hardcover)
Subjects: LCSH: Devotional exercises. | Christian life.
Classification: LCC BV4832.3 .V69 2018 | DDC 248.8/6—dc23 LC record available at https://lccn.loc
.gov/2017047623

Any Internet addresses (websites, blogs, etc.) and telephone numbers in this book are offered as a resource.
They are not intended in any way to be or imply an endorsement by Zondervan, nor does Zondervan vouch
for the content of these sites and numbers for the life of this book.

The names and details of some individuals depicted here have been changed to protect anonymity.

Published in association with William K. Jensen Literary Agency, 119 Bampton Court, Eugene, Oregon 97404.

Cover design: Curt Diepenhorst
Cover photography: Mary Anne Morgan
Author photo: Hope Voskamp
Interior design: Kait Lamphere

First printing January 2018 / Printed in the United States of America

To my beautiful mama, Linda—
whose name actually means beautiful—
because God knew right from the
beginning who you would be.

CONTENTS

PART THREE:

How Do You Let Your Broken Heart Receive?

PART FOUR:

How Can the Brokenhearted
Find Real Communion?

PART FIVE:

How Can the Brokenhearted Release Control?

PART SIX:

How Do the Brokenhearted Get to Love?

INTRODUCTION

Men of the breaking hearts had a quality about them not known to or understood by common men. They habitually spoke with spiritual authority. They had been in the Presence of God and they reported what they saw there.

A. W. TOZER, *THE PURSUIT OF GOD*

There are a million stars, a trillion, flung across the summer sky, a million more than any of us can count.

The night sky can seem close over the farm.

There are nights over our fields that it feels like we could grab the Big Dipper itself and ladle up light. There are nights that can feel bathed in abundant light.

When the Perseid meteor shower falls in mid-August, we spread blankets out by the edge of the stilled and drowsing wheat fields and watch for streaming fireballs of light to fall into our waiting hope. Some nights we just sit at the edge of the farm porch, sit at the edge of all the things that have gone wrong in a day, and watch the courage of stars, blazing brave in the dark.

Sitting together under a blanket of stars, one of the kids muttered it, "What are stars made of? Where does all that light come from?"

I tried to remember what I'd read in one of my old science textbooks, tried to explain it slowly so they'd listen, remember, what stars really are.

"Stars are made from explosions and collisions of elements. Stars are made from a breaking at their center. Which allows for a process called nuclear fusion, a process that releases an enormous amount of energy, of light."

I murmur it again, because how have I never seen the stars quite like that? Stars are made from a continuous breaking. And it's the gravitational friction of this breaking that makes them bright.

Breaking—then blazing.

This is always the abundant way of the universe.

Brokenness multiplies into abundance. This seems impossible—unlikely. And this is the unfailing way of God. Multiplication *happens out of brokenness*. And the sum is abundant life.

Stars are the scars of the sky—made into the light of the world.

What would happen if the scars you carry are what God uses to carry Christ to a scarred and broken world?

Weak is the real strong.

Brokenness is the real abundance.

Breaking—then blazing.

Dying—then rising.

Trust the abundant ways of the universe, the ways of Almighty God.

Scars are but stars that let His light burn through the night. Stars and scars are signs that point The Way.

I never told the kids that the brightest stars are known as supernovas. That when a star dies, it sends out a massive shock wave, that the death of the star is known as a supernova explosion, appearing in the night sky many times brighter than the surrounding stars.

Die to pride, die to self, die to agendas, die to comfort, die to ease—and your life explodes with abundant life. Unexpectedly, the secret to abundance is not about self—but about *dying* to self.

For the holy sake of our blessed sanity, we've got to go lose ourselves so we can find ourselves. *Breaking—then blazing.*

That's what this book is about.

These pages are about the wildly abundant life found in wildly unexpected places. These pages are about taking the dare to journey into a deeply meaningful life. The abundant life isn't found in what's touted as the good life bought on credit; it's found in the upside-down life, in broken places, with broken people, being most near the broken heart of Christ. Abundance is found in the loaves being broken and given, in the seed being broken open to new life, in the stars breaking—then blazing . . . in all the bits of our broken hearts. Abundance isn't about having as much as you want—abundance is about having as much of God as you want.

The starry night sky can feel like heaven has drawn near over our farm fields, over our upturned, seeking faces.

Out of the greatest brokenness, you can most greatly experience God's nearness.

It's okay. It's really okay. There are nights I step out on the porch, look up, and . . . just exhale.

Do not ever be afraid of broken things—this is the beginning of abundant things.

The stars bear witness.

Maybe all fear of loss, of not enough, of scarcity, of lack of abundance is but the notion that God's love ends. But when does His love ever end?

The stars go on forever, infinitely, over the farm.

When you step into our house from the farm's front porch, you can see it hanging over our old barn beam table, a canvas of lit and colored squares that suggest Christ hanging on the cross. They call Him that—the Bright Morning Star. His hands reach out in surrendered givenness. Christ takes the form of meaningfulness: cruciform.

There's a journey toward deep meaningfulness that beckons, a way of seeing, a way of stars, of the Bright Morning Star, that changes everything, and the soul can't help but ask:

Where did all this light come from?

Part One

How Can the Brokenhearted Keep Going?

Devotion 1

DECISIVE GIVENNESS

*Walk in the way of love, just as Christ loved us and gave
himself up for us as a fragrant offering and sacrifice to God.*

EPHESIANS 5:2

When I saw the billboard plastered on a wall somewhere in the city, it brought me up short. I stepped back to take it in, stood there in front of it like a fool farm hick.

Blazoned across the three panels like a wake-up call: "Why do you get out of bed in the morning?" And three images: some daredevil plunges off his surfboard—FEAR OF FAILURE. An astronaut latches himself in for launch—THE NEED TO SUCCEED. Some guy holds a curling cat—THE LOVE OF YOUR LIFE.

So why in the world *do* you get out of bed in the morning? I'm pretty sure I don't bother getting out of bed for any purring feline, and no, I don't have any rocket ship or this hankering to go launching off into the cosmos. And, quite frankly, I've never had the guts to take on any looming wave while trying to balance on a death-defying sliver of wobbling fiberglass.

But standing there before the billboard and its haunting question and it comes as a beat under my feet, a rhythm down the street, the question begging an answer. I want to accost the steady stream of blank-faced commuters rushing past me and ask them if they know. I want to ask old men on park benches and kids on park swings and mamas at sinks with young ones slung up on tired hips, and the brave who get out of bed all alone and face their own uphill road: *Why—why, you with your broken heart, why do you bother to keep getting out of bed?*

Do you find your feet because you're driven by a relentless fear of failure, or beaten down by the need to succeed? Or do you hit the floor for the love of a ball of fur?

Because this is what I know: Nothing is more necessary than finding God and falling in love and deeper into Him. Love decides. Love decides everything. What you are in love with decides what you live for. What you are in love with decides what you get out of bed for.

Fall in love with His hands that shaped your heart, that cup your face, that trace your scars, that caress you with grace. Fall in love with His face in a thousand faces, in the baby who meets you at the crib rail, and the teenager who doesn't want to budge, and that man who never fails to put feet to the floor and find his Levi jeans and head out the back door to brave the hardworking world for love.

Fall in love with the One who fills your lungs with this breath and all these people and this sky and all this light, all this glorious light.

You have to fall in love because this will get you up and keep you going every day. Because love decides. And love isn't about agreeing with someone; it's about sacrificing for someone. Love is givenness. Love is surrender. Love is living broken and given like bread.

Love decides everything, which is another way of saying, *sacrifice* is the essence of everything. Fall in love, fall into sacrifice, and you will always rise. Go fall in love with grace and mercy and the only One who has ever loved you to death—and back to the realest, abundant life. Because the world is begging us all to get out of bed and live given, get out of bed and sacrifice for someone hurting, for someone different, for someone forgotten or marginalized, to hold the hand of someone who doesn't look like us, to lean in and listen to someone angry and grieving and doubting the likes of us, to give a bit of ourselves to those who feel like they aren't given much real space at the table.

Read the headlines, read your news feed, and then defy the dark and go fall in love with kids raised in different neighborhoods than yours. Fall in love with God in the faces that tell stories different than yours; fall in love with people who think and live and walk in circles far different than yours. Sacrifice for someone—so your sanity, your fulfillment, your abundant joy, isn't sacrificed.

Sacrifice will always leave you the most satisfied. Fall in love, stay in love, stay sacrificing, and you live the most satisfied. *What you are in love with in your life decides everything about your life. Love decides everything.*

The sun can rise, and we all could rise, falling around each other, falling all around, healing, rising.

FOR REFLECTION

✧ How is God now asking you to see your brokenness today?
✧ What would abundance look like in your life today?

Devotion 2

In Brokenness, Abundant Light

"He himself bore our sins" in his body on the cross, so that we might die to sins and live for righteousness; "by his wounds you have been healed."

1 PETER 2:24

Sometimes you can feel the crush of it on your brittle rib cage. Great grief isn't made to fit inside your body. It's why your heart breaks. If you haven't felt this yet, it is likely, by His severe and surgical mercy, that someday you will.

There's absolutely no tidy pattern as to who gets pain and who gets peace. How had I not seen that the brokenness of this world is so all-encompassing that it encompasses all of us?

The wheat stands behind the orchard, turning itself into pure gold.

This is the deal we all get: guaranteed suffering. It is coming, unstoppable, like time.

There are graves coming, there is dark coming, there is heartbreak coming. We are not in control, and we never were. One moment you're picking up balls of crusty, dirty socks strewn across the bedroom floor, and the next moment you're picking up the pieces of your shattered life.

How do you live with a broken heart?

All the wheat looks like an onyx sea. The trees at the edge of the field reach up like a lyric scratched across the sky. It's like that line of Hugo's from *Les Misérables*: "There is a spectacle grander than the sea, and that is the sky; there is a spectacle grander than the sky, and it is the interior of the soul."[1] How does the interior of your soul live with broken things, through broken things?

Jesus died crying.

Jesus died of a broken heart. Those words were still warm on His cracked lips: "My God, my God, why have you forsaken me?"[2] The movement of a life of faith is always toward answering that singular question. Read the headlines. Read the obituaries. Read people's eyes. Isn't the essence of the Christian life to answer that one, nail-sharp question: *God, why in this busted-up world have You abandoned me?*

I can see that question hanging over our farm table, up in the gable, from that framed canvas of a thousand little broken squares of color. In the semiabstract painting, there's no tidy pattern, just light and dark bleeding into this subtle suggestion of Jesus hanging on the cross. He's hoarse with the begging, for Himself, for us: "God, why have You abandoned me?" And He surfaces in the patches of color, the broken brushstrokes, the silhouette of Him visible in the chaos—Christ entering all this chaos.

There is the truth: Blessed—lucky—are those who cry. Blessed are those who are sad, who mourn, who feel the loss of what they love—because they will be held by the One who loves them. There is a strange and aching happiness only the hurting know—for they shall be held.

And, by God, we're the hurting beggars begging: Be close to the brokenhearted. Save the crushed in spirit. Somehow make suffering turn this evil against itself, so that a greater life rises from the dark. *God, somehow.*

I was eighteen, with scars across my wrists, when I heard a pastor tell a whole congregation that he had once "lived next to a loony bin." I'd looked at the floor when everyone laughed. They didn't know how I had left my only mama behind the locked doors of psychiatric wards more than a few times. When they laughed, I felt the blood drain away from my face, and I'd wanted to stand up and howl, "It is not the healthy who need a doctor, but the sick."[3]

I'd wanted to stand up and beg: When the church isn't for the suffering and broken, then the church isn't for Christ. Because Jesus, with His pierced side, is always on the side of the broken. Jesus always moves into places moved with grief. Jesus always seeks out where the suffering is, and that's where Jesus stays. The wound in His side proves that Jesus is always on the side of the suffering, the wounded, the busted, the broken.

I believed this then and believe it now and I'd say I know it to be true—but there is more than believing; there is living what you believe. *Do I really?*

What I wanted that Sunday when I was eighteen, sitting in a church of laughter mocking the hurting, was for all the broken to say it together, as one body, to say it for the hurting and broken and to say it to each other, because there is not even one of us who hasn't lost something, who doesn't fear something, who doesn't ache with some unspoken pain. I wanted us to say it to each other until it is the bond of a promise we cannot break:

The body of Christ doesn't offer you some clichés, but something to cling to—right here in our own scarred hands.

His body doesn't offer some platitudes, but some place for your pain—right here in our own offered time.

His body doesn't offer some excuses, but we'll be an example—right here in our bending down and washing your wounds.

And we are His and He is ours, so we are each other's, and we will never turn away.

But instead I'd heard preached what Jesus never had—some pseudo-good news that if you just pray well, sing well, worship well, live well, and give lots, well, you get to take home a mind and body that are well. *That's not how the complex beauty of life breaks open.*

The real Jesus turns to our questions of why—why this brokenness, why this darkness?—and says, "You're asking the wrong question. You're looking for someone to blame. There is no such cause-effect here."[4] "This happened so the power of God could be seen in him."[5]

There's brokenness that's not about blame. There's brokenness that makes a canvas for God's light to be lavishly splashed across the darkness. There's brokenness that carves windows straight into our souls.

Brokenness cracks open a soul so the power of God can crack the darkness in the world.

FOR REFLECTION

- ✧ How might God be working redemptively through the brokenness in your life?
- ✧ Where are you seeing His abundant light right now?

Devotion 3

WINGING TOWARD ABUNDANCE

*Dear friends, let us love one another, for love comes from
God. Everyone who loves has been born of God and knows
God. Whoever does not love does not know God, because
God is love.*

1 JOHN 4:7–8

I once held a bird in my hand.

No one else could see its brave heart, but I felt it. I felt its heart thumping hard and afraid and beating bravely still.

It happens—there are ways to look fine on the outside . . . and no one knows what you've really survived.

But the truth is? You didn't just survive, so let's toss that myth out right at the outset.

The way you keep walking? You may be wounded. You may be hurting. You may be limping. You may feel alone and overwhelmed and an unspoken broken—but you're no victim.

You're not just a survivor. You're a thriver.

You may bleed—but you rise.

Yeah, it may not feel like it—but you are seen . . . how you just keep keeping your chin up and limping brave through the hurt and how you keep taking one step out of bed and another step through the door—and how you keep scaling mountains by relentlessly taking steps *forward*.

But I wanted you to know your wounds are seen and you are going to be okay—it is all going to be okay.

Not that you badge-flash your scars or anything.

Or try to hide them, ashamed.

It's just sometimes there's this passing flicker in your eyes, old pain shooting white right through.

But mostly, quietly, the scars just become you—become who you are and become you . . . make you more beautiful—they just become the way your skin pulls mottled and raised over your soul and this is how you fit most beautifully.

How you can look healed and thickened and still feel so stretched paper-thin? Yeah, I know.

If someone brushed by you just a certain way? You'd be blue, tender and sore all over again, or just spill without a sound.

Inside, the warrior is small.

The kingdom of heaven belongs to such as these.

I just wanted to reach out and touch, glance at your wounds. You don't have to say anything. Explain anything, excuse anything. I just wanted to touch them, acknowledge them. *Acknowledge you.* Bless them, you, without even a sound—only eyes that make you feel seen . . . deeply known.

I just wanted to whisper your way: Wounded warriors win. There is no remission of sins or the crossing of finish lines without things getting bloody.

You are so brave to keep facing the light. To keep walking toward Home.

The scarred Savior will know you're His by your own scars.

And when He cups your face, that moment when His scars touch your skin? *You'll be wholly healed.*

Hang on. Press in. Look up.

Can I just whisper? I know you must feel like people, the church, have

25

wanted you to go away. Sweep your scars under the proverbial rug. *Erase you, avoid you, silence you.*

Because it's too uncomfortable for us, the neighbors, the church, the body, to face our own culpability in scars. Face our own fallen disfigurement. *Pollyanna wasn't the only one who wore rose-colored glasses.* Few like to admit that we come from a long line of Roman soldiers who have crucified our own.

I know—*and I'm sorry.* When it comes to the bloodied and wounded, we suddenly all become like turtles, lose our thin, bare necks and shirk back into our see-nothing shells. Who sticks out their necks for the broken and wounded? Only the One who stretched out His arms infinitely wide and had them nailed there so you would never doubt that His love was going anywhere.

Sometimes the church doesn't want to know details or listen to wounds, weep, or wade into the bloody mess. Christ is the truth, but too many of His people run from the truth.

Yet if Christ is the truth, then where there isn't truth, there isn't Christ. *Why ever be afraid of the truth?* If we believe in the sovereign grace of God, the redemptive restoration of God, then we need never fear the broken things.

And maybe—maybe our deafening silence sometimes in the body, in the church, is just this: Truth necessitates confrontation—and a whole lot of us are more chicken than Christian. Sometimes we'd rather save our own skin than the skin of the bruised and battered and beaten. *We can be more in love with self-preservation than with Savior-glorification.*

Sometimes as communities, churches, families—we'd rather make pain invisible than say injustice is intolerable. So the injustice continues.

So we pretend you, the wounded and brokenhearted, don't exist, so we can pretend the sin that caused this wound doesn't exist—because ultimately, our actions prove it: *we don't really think the Wounded Healer exists.*

We act like we forget that God can raise up phoenixes from ashes—and that this is His business, *this is what He does.* That which we refuse to thank Christ for, we refuse to believe Christ can redeem.

Wounded one, brokenhearted thriver—you gotta believe there's a whole lot of us who believe. A whole lot of us are getting to our feet and sticking out our necks because we long to be like Christ who stretched out His arms, we long to be like Christ, cruciform—and we want you to know: *we want you.* You, not masked . . . you, not prettified, but you with your messy scars and your tender blue places and all that just-below-the-skin hurt.

Because when we ignore suffering, we ignore the suffering Savior.

We need you. We need the wounded, we need the limping, we need the hurting, we need the broken and messy—you are us. We need to cup your tears, to water hard and crusted places, or there's no growth in the kingdom of God.

We need your raw story or we lose any hope of the redemptive Story. We need to hold your broken heart *or we have no heart.*

Can I just say: *I am sorry.* I am sorry for how alone you have felt. *How abandoned, how ignored.* We need you. It is the wounded ones who make us heal. And it is the hurting ones who make us honest; it's the broken ones who put us back together again.

And it is the scarred ones who make the body of Christ sensitive.

Once, it's true, we found a trapped and wounded bird. And when we simply cupped it close and listened to its heart—we saw the way of abundance with our own eyes. We saw how that bird turned toward the light and flew.

For Reflection

- ✧ Where might you see brokenhearted suffering around you today that God is calling you not to ignore?
- ✧ How might lack of forgiveness be keeping you from living into abundance today?

Devotion 4

THE BROKENHEARTED WAY

Therefore, there is now no condemnation for those who are in Christ Jesus, because through Christ Jesus the law of the Spirit who gives life has set you free from the law of sin and death.

ROMANS 8:1–2

I wash and dry the white porcelain pitcher at the sink. That moment, the edges of me feel fragile. Not wanting one more thing to crack. Not wanting to crack one thing more.

Is there a grace that can bury the fear that your faith isn't big enough and your faults are too many? A grace that washes your dirty wounds and wounds the devil's lies? A grace that embraces you before you prove anything—and after you've done everything wrong? A grace that holds you when everything is breaking down and falling apart—and whispers that everything is somehow breaking free and falling together?

I had wanted someone to reach over to me at eighteen, sit in that church pew next to me, someone to touch my shoulder, to steady things, and to say, "Shame is a bully, but grace is a shield. You are safe here."

What if the busted and broken hearts could *feel* there's a grace that holds us and calls us beloved and says we belong and no brokenness ever has the power to break us away from being safe? What if we *experienced* the miracle of grace that can touch all our wounds?

I wanted to write it on walls and on the arms scarred with wounds, make it the refrain we sing in the face of the dark and broken places: No shame. No fear. No hiding. All's grace. It's always safe for the suffering here. You can struggle and you can wrestle and you can hurt, and we will be here. Grace will meet you here; grace, perfect comfort, will always be served here.

How do you remember there's a Doctor in the house who "binds up the brokenhearted,"[6] a Wounded Healer who uses nails to buy freedom and crosses to resurrect hope, and He never treats those who hurt on the inside as less than those who hurt on the outside? How do you remember that "hearts are broken in ten thousand ways, for this is a heart-breaking world; and Christ is good at healing all manner of heart-breaks"?[7] How do you stand a thousand nights out on the creaking porch, lean over the pine rail, and look up: The same hand that unwraps the firmaments of winging stars wraps liniments around the wounded heart; the One whose breath births galaxies into being births healing into the heart of the broken.

I put the porcelain pitcher on the barn board shelf by the farm table. All of us in a heart-breaking world, we are the fellowship of the broken like that painting of Jesus over the table. Over all of us is the image of the wounded God, the God who breaks open and bleeds with us.

How do you live with your one broken heart? All I can think is—only the wounds of God can heal our wounds. This is the truth, and I feel the rising of it: Suffering is healed by suffering; wounds are healed by wounds. It jars me, shatters my fears into the softness of Him: Bad brokenness is healed by His good brokenness. *Bad brokenness is broken by good brokenness.*

What in the world does that even mean? And could I find out simply by daring to discover it?

Dare I look for a brokenhearted way to . . . abundance?

FOR REFLECTION

✧ How have you been living with your one broken heart?

✧ How is God asking you to step toward an abundant healing?

Devotion 5

VULNERABLE GIVENNESS

Continue to work out your salvation with fear and trembling,
for it is God who works in you to will and to act in order to
fulfill his good purpose.

PHILIPPIANS 2:12–13

I go out to the wheat fields to ride a few rounds with the kid in the
tractor. He tells me about all the mistakes he made, how he jammed
the grain buggy auger and they spent twenty-seven minutes unplugging
it (he timed it) and how they had to pail up the wheat that spilled like his
blatant failure there at the end of the field.

He bit his lip hard, trying to stop what he could feel coming, and I
turn away to give the boy time to be brave.

He says how he drove in too high a gear going uphill, how he stalled
the tractor and ended up jackknifing the wagon and tractor real bad by
the bottom of the hill. I nod, but I don't say what I feel: Going in high
gear without enough soul fuel will stall and jackknife your life every single
time, Son.

He's been working long days and into the night, running the tractor
alongside his dad in the combine; his younger sister, Shalom, she's running
the auger on the home farm; and his brother, Levi, he's hauling wagons
full of wheat from each farm back to Shalom and the bins.

There's a lot of happiness in this world that depends on being brave

31

enough to keep working when it'd be easier to quit. Nothing good gets started without getting to work—and nothing great gets finished without staying at the work.

The kids are learning it far deeper than the cerebral level, down in their aching muscles: laziness looks like a friend, but only work can invite you home.

"I don't know if I can be a farmer, Mama." Malakai leans over from the steering wheel, whispers it to me quiet as the tractor idles. "Don't know if I'm tough enough for everything that you get wrong."

Oh, Son—*don't I know that*. And I lay my hand gently on the back of the boy's slender neck. Sometimes only a handful of words reach out and touch you with their heart. Yeah, kid, we work, but not as ones who do not know the relief of grace. We work hard, but not as ones who grow hardened. What we're ultimately always working out is our own salvation.

"You know . . ." I run my hand through Kai's mess of curls. "We all get things wrong, things seem to go wrong, even—or mostly—*we* are wrong. But it's not about growing tough enough to take what life throws at you; it's about staying *open enough* to all of life to simply *receive* it."

In all of our work, maybe what we're most working out is the vulnerable grace of our salvation. It's not about growing tough for life; it's about growing open to life as it comes—and spiritually, vulnerably, growing through.

How do you remember that this is one of the most important things in life? To thrive, you must surrender to a kind of openness. You must surrender control and trust One who is in control, though you will be taken beyond what you can control and into a kind of brokenness, a brokenness that will hurt and yet be kind. A painful grace.

This is being truly alive: surrender unshielded to the unknown—because there is a deeper Love that is knowable.

And it is only possible to know the touch of His deeper love when you live without armor, vulnerable, exposed. Yes, never stop working

32

hard—but don't grow tough. Because at the end of the day? Jesus wants our worship more than our work.

It's an old and elemental truth: you are made of dust because you are made to grow.

You were made to feel, you were made to bend vulnerable in wind, you were made to reach for the sun. It's what the fields of wheat say: you were made to grow, and that only happens if you are fragile and brave enough to break.

Sure, life and people will try to tell you loudly that you need to be like a rock, that you'll need to harden up to live in a harsh world, be impenetrable, unmoved. But no one can really live the abundant life that way. *Rocks don't breathe.* Because they're dead.

It's the thin-skinned wheat that bravely breathes in its own way.

It's tender stalks that are deeply rooted so they can reach for sun.

Rocks are invulnerable.

And wheat is fragile.

And one is perfectly dead, and one is exquisitely alive.

Humanity's particular beauty is only possible because of its fragility. Your beauty is not in your formidableness, but in your fragility.

I tell Kai this. The boy brims and nods and he's a mess like his mother, but he takes me anyway.

When you already have a Rock, you can live the beauty of being a vulnerable, growing thing.

Malakai hauls wheat wagons till 9:30 on a Saturday night and then heads to the barn and feeds a couple hundred sows. The Farmer Husband and Levi finish up in the field, get the wagons away, the auger down, the bin sealed up, all the tractors home and in the shed, and drag in the back door sometime between 11:50 p.m. and the Lord's Day, a twenty-hour workday for them.

There is light in their givenness. In the way the work of all the people can be given for the harvest. We can do hard and holy things, break and give ourselves like bread, and our lives can become an abundant feast. All our small work together is what does big and beautiful work in the world.

We can open up rock-hard places and bend, to give in the wind of the Spirit. There are days you can see it, in all the ditches and along all the roads, the fragile stalks growing in the silvered light.

For Reflection

✧ Where might God be working to soften your heart today in the midst of your work?

✧ Where might there be hardness in your heart that is hindering your growth into the abundant life?

Devotion 6

BREAKING BROKENNESS

And he took bread, gave thanks and broke it, and gave it
to them.

LUKE 22:19

I had first read it slowly, years ago—how in the original language
"gave thanks" reads *eucharisteo*. The root word of *eucharisteo* is
charis, meaning "grace." Jesus took the bread and saw it as grace and
gave thanks.

If *eucharisteo* had been the first dare, the first journey of discovery into
a life of letting God love me and counting all those ways, could this be a
dare for the next leg of the journey, the way leading higher up and deeper
in, daring me to let all the not-enough there in my open hands—let it be
broken into more than enough? A dare to let all my brokenness be made
into abundance. *Break and give away. The broken way.*

What if this was the safest embrace—the way of being wanted and
held and found in the midst of falling apart? What did Jesus do? In His last
hours, in His abandonment, Jesus doesn't look for comfort or try to shield
Himself against the rejection; He breaks the temptation to self-protect—and
gives the vulnerability of Himself. In the sharp edge of grief, Jesus doesn't
look for something to fill the broken and alone places; He takes and gives
thanks—and then does the most countercultural thing: He doesn't keep
or hoard or hold on—but breaks and gives away. In the midst of intimate

35

betrayal, He doesn't defend or drown Himself in addicting distractions; He breaks and is given—He gives His life.

Because what else is life-giving?

Out of the fullness of the grace that He has received, He thanks, and breaks, and gives away—and He makes a way for life-giving communion. A broken way.

How does this make any rational sense? It doesn't. But maybe that's the only way you ever know the greatest truths: The greatest truths always are the greatest paradox. And what could be a greater paradox than this? Out of feeling lavishly loved by God, one can break and give away that lavish love—and know the complete fullness of love.

The miracle happens in the breaking.

Somehow . . . the miracle of communion, oneness, wholeness, abundance, it happens in the exact opposite—in breaking and giving.

Somehow . . . the miracle, the intimacy, of communion comes through brokenness.

What if a kind of communion is found in a trinity of brokenness— through broken places and broken people and being broken and given.

When our own brokenness meets the brokenness of the world, don't we enter into and taste the brokenness and givenness of Christ? And isn't this the actual abundant wholeness of communion?

Somehow I wonder if it's in shattered places, with broken people, we are most near the broken heart of Christ.

What if we only find our whole selves through this mystery—the mystery of death and resurrection, of brokenness and abundance? Could this be what it means to live in the encircling embrace of communion: brokenness giving way to abundance—and then abundance, which is then broken and given . . . gives way to an ever greater abundance? I think this is the ring of the fellowship of communion.

Is this way realest life—or is life really this way? Am I saving myself . . . or dying—or both?

36

Why are we afraid of broken things? I can think of a thousand raw reasons. But touch the broken and the hungry and the hurting and the thirsty and the busted, and you touch a bit of Christ. *Why are we afraid of suffering?*

What if the abundance of communion is only found there in the brokenness of suffering—because suffering is where God lives?

Suffering is where God gives the most healing intimacy.

FOR REFLECTION

✧ Why have you been afraid of broken things?
✧ How might God be asking you to experience the abundance of communion with Him through the brokenness of suffering?

RE-MEMBERING
THE BROKEN

"Do this in remembrance of me."

LUKE 22:19

A preacher's words had grabbed me by the lazy jugular: "Jesus took bread and broke it and said to do this in remembrance of Me—and this is the one and only command Christ gave to do continually, over and over again."

"To do," the Greek word *poieo*, is a present imperative, and the present tense indicates continuing action; thus it could be translated "continue to do this." Continue to do this literally, with bread and wine—and continuously do this with your life, with the bread of your moments, the wine of your days.

This is the practice Jesus gave for us to continually practice our faith, to practice again and again. In remembrance of Him. Continuously do this at the sink, at the stove, at the street corner, at the setting of the sun and at its rising again, and never stop continuously doing this.

Did I know anything about this? How was I doing the one command Christ asked to do continuously?

And continuously do what? Remember Me. We, the people with chronic soul amnesia, are called to be *the re-membering people*. The people who remember—and have their brokenness re-membered.

The shaft of light falling across the floor, falling across my feet—it's fractured by shadows from beyond the window.

Remembrance—it comes from the Greek word *anamnesis*. The only four times this word *anamnesis* is used in Scripture, it is in reference to the sacrifice that Christ made and is "remembered" in the Last Supper (Luke 22:19; 1 Corinthians 11:24, 25; Hebrews 10:3).

I read once that *anamnesis* was a term used to express an intangible idea moving into this material, tangible world. The philosopher Plato had used the word *anamnesis* to express a remembering that allowed the world of ideas to impact the world of our everyday, allowing something in another world to take form in this physical one.

That was the point: remembrance, *anamnesis*, does not simply mean memory by mental recall, the way you remember your own address—but it means to experience a past event again through the physical, to make it take form through reenactment. Like the way you remember your own grandma Ruth by how your great-aunt Lois laughs, how she makes butterscotch squares for Sunday afternoons too, how she walks in her Birkenstocks with that same soft heel as Grandma did, her knees cracking up the stairs the same way too. The way your great-aunt Lois acts makes you remember in ways that make your grandma Ruth real and physically present again now.

There's a cupping grace to it—how remembering becomes a healing. We welcome remembering, we hold remembering, we let remembering wrap around us and carry us like a dance that need not end.

We are never abandoned when we hold on to remembrance.

Gabriel García Márquez scratched it down once, like words sealed in a bottle and sent back to the world: "What matters in life is not what happens to you but what you remember and how you remember it."[8]

That's it. What matters in your life is not so much what happens to you but what you happen to remember—and how that will influence how your life happens. What and how you remember will determine if your broken, dis-membered places will re-member you.

So how to continuously re-member? Re-member your broken and busted heart, remember Him crucified and who you are and your real name: the beloved.

Continuously do *this* in remembrance of Me.

The truth of *anamnesis* is to make Me [Christ] present. That's the truth of what He was saying: "Continuously make Me present." How in the world do you make Christ visibly present through this shattered chaos?

Be broken and given in a thousand common and uncommon ways. Live given a thousand times a day. Die a thousand little deaths. This feels like a dare that is choosing me. I don't know if I know how to do this. I don't know if I want to do this.

Maybe—there is no breaking of bad brokenness unless His people become good brokenness. But what do I know about the Via Dolorosa? What do I know of this suffering and sacrifice of the broken way?

The sun pools. The floor lights, everything lights—there is no physical body of Christ here on earth but ours. We are now Christ's only earthly body—and if we aren't the ones broken and given, we are the ones who dis-member Christ's body. Unless we are the ones broken and given, we incapacitate Christ's body on earth.

FOR REFLECTION

✧ How might your life look different if you continuously, moment by moment, consciously chose to make Christ present, if you lived broken and given like bread?

✧ How might you change what you are choosing to re-member so you can experience more of the abundant life?

Devotion 8

SACRIFICIAL GIVENNESS

This is love: not that we loved God, but that he loved us and
sent his Son as an atoning sacrifice for our sins.

1 JOHN 4:10

When I carry her into the ER the first time, with that brave, broken half heart of hers, the doctor asks me point-blank: *How did she get into this country?*

I keep it brief, to the point: "Love got her here."

And I don't mean what he thinks I mean.

Yeah, I don't tell the doctor about that ten-thousand-kilometer flight from Beijing across the top of the world. That there was a letter of approval from Immigration and the Ministry of Child and Family Services; there was nearly a year of relentlessly pounding paperwork and a million brave people in agencies and departments who locked arms to make a bridge from us to her—because none of that is the long and short of it, really.

Love got her here. Love got all of us here.

And yeah, you bet, folks can yell across aisles and Facebook streams at the other and the different and the loudly opinionated with an opinion far different from ours, but somewhere along the line, we're all the same kind of different with the same kind of story:

Love made us all, and love is what got us all here.

Which is another way of saying: sacrifice got us all here.

Someone sacrificed something, and someone, to get us all here in this country. Someone loved something more than themselves and sacrificed safety and ease and comfort and climbing higher up some flimsy ladder, so you could get to live in this country. Someone sacrificed shavings off their own heart to get you into this relationship, this marriage, this community, this place right now.

And I hold our broken and brave baby right there at my shoulder, her hands clutching strands of my hair, burying her head deeper into my neck, and I look around at a roomful of interns and doctors and surgeons and nurses with names like Cheruvadi and Maricor and Dipchand, and we're a nation of sacrificers.

A nation of givers and gifters and sacrificers and reachers, people who give when it costs and step up to lay it all down and choose to take less to give more.

People who know: the foundation of anything worth anything is always sacrifice.

Because the real truth tellers and freedom dwellers believe that when things are crumbling, when foundations are giving away, when relationships and hopes and dreams and countries and our world feel like it's falling apart—there is only one shape the pieces of our brokenness can take to know wholeness—and that is the shape of the cross.

If your healing doesn't look like a sacrificial cross—it isn't healing and it won't heal your soul. If your country, your relationships, your choices don't look like a sacrificial cross—you will end up dying in a thousand ways that never even crossed your mind.

You fit into the abundant life, the life you ultimately want—when you live shaped like a cross. Cruciform. Sacrificing.

And you can say all you want about love and sacrifice and choosing a truth-telling life, but your truth about love, it isn't the whole truth if it doesn't look like the sacrifice of the cross.

The only form real happiness can ever take is cruciform. The only way

42

to break free into the abundant life—is to live broken and given. Because life's not about choosing a lifestyle, but a way to serve.

In the middle of the night she cries for me from her crib—and from our bed, I reach for her. And our hands meet—and she laces her fingers tight through mine . . . And that's all she needs.

What dark places and hard times need us all to do is reach out and hold on.

She pulls my hand up to her face and cups my face in her hands. She lies there cupping my face between her hands, slow sleep breaths warming my face. I kiss her forehead the gentlest.

Love got us all here.

Sacrifice got us all here.

You have got to sacrifice something for someone—or you will have nothing and no one. Because without sacrifice—*we have nothing.*

And there are seven things a country, relationship, or life cannot have:

✧ power without principle
✧ money without work
✧ work without meaning
✧ comfort without conscience
✧ leadership without character
✧ love without sacrifice
✧ abundance without Christ

It's not necessary to feel great for a country or a relationship or a life to be great; it's only necessary to greatly sacrifice.

The doctor ends up saying her broken heart needs surgery soon, that she needs deep healing.

And I nod—healing. There's a way, for all of us. A way through brokenness.

I listen to it in the dark, her heart, one brave, sacrificial beat after another—steady and sure of the healing coming.

FOR REFLECTION

✧ How have you been mentored by the people in your life who have lived broken and given and sacrificed so that you are where you are?

✧ What do you need to sacrifice, or how do you need to live sacrificially, to more fully experience the true way of abundance?

Devotion 9

LIVING CRUCIFORM

A bruised reed he will not break,
and a smoldering wick he will not snuff out.

ISAIAH 42:3

There's this black pen lying on the table across from me. I pick up the pen and turn my wrist over. How many years had I cut that paling wrist, wearing my brokenness on the outside? I pick up the pen and on a whim—on a conviction, kind of ridiculously desperate to remember the radical symbolism, to remember the union, the communion—I write it on my wrist, let it bleed like a vow right there into the thin white skin: one little black cross.

I am busted and His, and He is broken and given and mine.

I trace that one black cross: Can you dare to break yourself into a kind of communion, a kind of union? Can you let the way be made for broken places to re-member?

This is one wild dare to live cruciform, to let life become shaped like a cross. This could be a dare to let life be shaped like union.

It's a dare to be married to mysteries so Christ has hands again in this world—and specifically mine.

This cross is a sign of my believing, that I am "called into the *koinonia* of His Son, Jesus Christ."⁹ I know this. The *eucharisteo* precedes the miracle, and the miracle is always, always *koinonia*. But maybe I haven't been living it long enough yet?

I wash my paling face at the bathroom mirror. The woman in the mirror is a wide-eyed deer caught in the headlights, life running her down, and she's desperate to know: *How can you believe there is enough in you of any value? How do you believe there is enough of you to live given—and be wanted?*

The wheat in the fields needed this rain that's sheeting down like some upstairs plumbing let loose. The sky slides down the windowpane next to the bathroom mirror like something a bit busted.

I need these questions, need answers to fall, to grow something in me strong enough to withstand this broken life. If I want to truly **Give It Forward Today**, if I want to be the gift, don't I have to believe there's enough in me that's a gift to give forward? Maybe we believe in Jesus; we just don't always believe in Him *working in us.*

The cold tap water feels good splashed on my face, running down my neck. It feels strange, even wrong, to believe He could find any value in my tarnished brokenness. But didn't He, somehow? Didn't He believe it was worth redeeming, renewing, resurrecting, to make all into more than enough, in spite of my brokenness and through it? That cross on the wrist, wasn't it a sign of Jesus' believing? Isn't the cross a sign of Christ believing in us, believing that the busted are to be believed in? Which feels unbelievable.

The slowing rain seems like a bestowing, belief growing.

Lotion massaged slowly into dry and chapped palms. Rubbed into the broken creases across the backs of my hands. There was what an Orthodox Hasidic rabbi had said on a flight westward. He'd put his prayer shawl in the overhead compartment and sat down, sweeping aside the tassels dangling from his pockets. And somewhere over the mountains, the light thick above the clouds, the rabbi turned to me, mid-conversation: "Why do you people always say it's about having a strong belief in God? Who sits with the knowing that God's belief in you is even stronger than yours in Him?"

I'd put down my Styrofoam cup of black coffee and tried to read the rabbi's face. He'd leaned forward in his seat and tilted his head so he could look at me directly. "You may believe in God, but never forget—it's *God* who believes in *you*."

He looked out the window and pointed. "Every morning that the sun rises and you get to rise? That's God saying He believes in you, that He believes in the story He's writing through you. He believes in *you* as a gift the world *needs*."

Was I living my life like I fully believed *that*? Because if Christ is in you—can God ever stop believing in you? Because doesn't He always believe in Christ in you, believe in the redemptive story Christ is writing through you, believe in Christ working to make all things in you into a gift back to the world?

God's mercies are new every morning—not as an obligation to you, but as an affirmation of you.

At the rabbi's words I'd nodded slowly and instinctively reached my thumb over, tracing the faint cross rubbed into my left wrist. *Christ is in me—so God can't help but believe in me, because Christ is in me!*

An abundant communion.

FOR REFLECTION

✧ How would it change your life, your days, your heart, if you believed that because Jesus is in you and your brokenness, God believes in you, because He is working through you and your brokenness?

✧ Reflecting on Jesus, who offers new mercies to you, not as an obligation to you, but as an affirmation of you—what does abundant communion with Jesus look like today?

Devotion 10

HELD BROKENNESS

He remembers his covenant forever,
the promise he made, for a thousand generations.

PSALM 105:8

It's not when that package finally decides to show up in the mail, dragged in through a foot of lingering snow.

It's not when I happen to turn around at the sink and remember that pan broiling in the oven before it burns to a sacrificial crisp.

It's not when, for a blink in the choreographed cosmos, the stars all align and I can see the bottom of all the laundry baskets.

That's not when it's the best.

I mean, honestly, who really knows when it's the best?

What feels like a great failure on earth may be revealed as a great success in heaven. This changes everything for me on the hard days.

We can't really keep going around saying, "You know, everything is what it is"—because how do we know how things really are and how things are going to turn out to be?

But I will just go ahead and say—the moment in the early morning dark, when our littlest girl reaches, when she holds on to me, when her fingers stretch to find mine, when she finds and clenches tight, when I hear her breathing fall again into the rhythms of home and here and sleep—*that is the moment I best remember, try to memorize, to always remember.*

That's the moment that re-members me.

When life breaks our hearts, goes ahead and breaks parts and members of us—there are moments that can re-member us, that can put the parts and members of bits of our heart back together again.

Her holding on to me re-members me. Her holding on to me—makes Christ intimately present to me.

The dark feels lighter, us holding on to each other, her fingers tied gently around mine like the relief of peace.

Maybe there is always just holding on through the dark.

A mother looked me in the eye this week and told me her son hung himself and she was holding on to that cross on her wrist, to living cruciform, to following Him who is the Way, to finding the broken way through. We fell into each other, gripped each other's backs. Hope is faith holding on a moment longer.

There are women who can't remember the last time they were held, the last time they were pulled in close to another beating heart so they didn't feel alone.

There are women who can never remember being cupped the gentlest, their faces traced and outlined by a fingertip of love, who can't remember letting someone look long into their eyes without shame. *Who can't remember not looking away.*

There are hands that forget what it feels like *to simply be held*, forget what it feels like to be connected deeply to just one other human being on this spinning planet.

There are parents reaching for kids who are reaching for something else, reaching away. Dads reaching for kids who don't want to look back, kids reaching for dads who have never really looked long their way, siblings who can't find each other anymore and maybe don't even care, women reaching for lifelines and only finding deadlines and end of the lines.

It can be hard to hold on when you don't feel held.

The great challenge of faith is holding on to hope after you've lost your naïveté.

A heartbroken woman announces this week that her young husband and father of two died, ravaged with cancer. And she just shot straight with us: *not once did she reach out to any church's coffee bars, trendy lounges, and hipster ambience to help her hold on.*

When it's hard to hold on—no one holds on to what is cool. *They hold on to Christ.*

When it's hard to hold on, no one holds on to what is hipster. They hold on to Him who is holy and healing.

When it's hard to hold on—we don't hold on to trendy, *we hold on to the True Vine*; we don't hold on to the prevailing and popular, because we need to hold on to the Prince of Peace and the true Perfecter of our faith.

It's the beliefs we hold that hold on to us, even when we're struggling to hold on.

And we can always keep holding on because our God can always be counted on.

The art of living lies in the balance of holding on—and letting go because He's holding on to you. *He's holding on to everything.*

The art of living is about holding on to His promises—and surrendering to His plan.

Hold on to His promises.

Let go into His plan.

There are marriages holding on only by one fragile, fraying thread, and women holding on to thin hope by the skin of their teeth, and adoptive parents holding on by their whitened knuckles to just one more day, and parents of prodigals holding on when everything's telling them to hightail it off this insane ride.

And there she is, toddling over to me at the end of the day, when I'm standing there by the sink with its basin of tepid water, washing the last of the pots, and she looks up at me, both arms raised.

"Mama, Mama! Mama! Please, Mama, up. I hold you."

And I lean over. *"You want to hold me, Baby Girl?"* She nods, grins in her Cheshire-cat-spreading-smile way that melts me.

She actually wants *me* to pick *her* up, wants *me* to hold *her*—but the only words she knows for the holding that she wants are the words she's heard me say a thousand times: *"Come. I hold you."*

"Yes, Mama, please, up? *I hold you?*"

And I scoop her up—and the universe seems to jolt to a holy still—pause—and all us hangers-on, all us holding on, we exhale:

Yes, child, you can hold me—because I am holding you.

Yes, child, you can keep holding onto me—because I AM is always holding on to you.

And when she flings her arms around my neck, presses her love right into my cheek, I can feel it, the re-membering, parts of my broken heart re-membering—all of us the children can keep holding on—*because we are the ones always held.*

──────── FOR REFLECTION ────────

✧ How have you experienced the abundant embrace of God holding you through brokenness?

✧ Is what you are holding on to in your life and priorities causing more brokenness or abundance?

Part Two

How Do We Live Like the Brokenhearted, Cruciform Christ?

Devotion 11

RISKY LIVING

But he said to me, "My grace is sufficient for you, for my power is made perfect in weakness."

2 CORINTHIANS 12:9

When my dad called this morning, he said his farming friend, Alan Bertrand, was "just trying to figure out whether to spend the years he's got left restoring another one of those antique tractors he has out in the shop, or if he should spend the time he's got left trying to track down his daughter he hasn't seen or heard from in ten years."

I could see Dad in my mind in his suspender overalls. "And so, Alan decided?"

"The tractor. He already knew how to fix the tractor. Little risk. But the daughter? He doesn't even know where she is. That was *all* risk."

But, Dad, I wanted to say, *love is a risk . . . that's never a risk.*

"Look," Dad continued. "Do we give up what makes us really happy, whatever we are good at, a lifetime of happiness to risk our lives on a relationship that might never make us happy? There are no guarantees with people."

And before I could think, the words left my mouth. "Jesus said, 'Whoever loses their life for me will find it.'"[10]

Jesus risked Himself on me. How can I not risk my life on you? You may not love me back. You may humble me, humiliate me, reject me, shatter my heart, and drive the shards into my soul—but this is not the part that matters. What matters is that in the act of loving we become more like the givenness of Love Himself. What matters most is not if our love makes other people change, but that in loving, *we change*. What matters is that in the sacrificing to love someone, we become more like Someone. Regardless of anything or anyone else changing, the success of loving is in how we change because *we kept on loving.*

Who knew that sometimes if you don't risk anything—you're actually risking everything?

Love is always worth the risk because the *reward* of loving is in the *joy of loving* itself. *Love is a risk that's never a risk.* Loving itself is the greatest outcome because loving makes one more beautiful, more like brokenhearted Beauty Himself.

No matter what the outcome looks like, if your love has poured out, your life will be success-full.

Relationships are the realest reality—and the realest risk . . . and the worthiest risk. Because in sacrificing ourselves, we are guaranteed to discover the depths of our best and realest selves.

Whatever you love is what you really are. *Tractor—or daughter?* The saddest thing of all may be when we give away our lives to insignificant things. Why love the wrong things in the wrong ways? The only way to the abundant life is to love the *right* things in the *right* ways.

Could I turn to my people, any and all people, and live it? *I am what I love and I will love you like Jesus, because of Jesus, through the strength of Jesus.* I will love when I'm not loved back. I will love when I'm hurt and disappointed and betrayed and inconvenienced and rejected. I simply will love—no expectations, no conditions, no demands.

Nothing will stop me from loving—not time, distance, disappointment, or death. Nothing will stop me from the risk of vulnerably loving because love like this is not a risk.

Love defies logic and keeps on loving when it makes no sense because that is what love does.

And I will fall in love and fail at love and fall in my love, but I will never stop the practicing, practicing, practicing, the givenness and the receiving. For what is faith, what is love, if it is not practiced?

Giving away the heart . . . heals the heart.

FOR REFLECTION

✧ What are the priorities of your broken heart? As you prioritize what you love the most, how are these priorities a reflection of who you really are?

✧ How is your life proving that relationships are the realest reality . . . and the realest risk . . . and the worthiest risk?

Devotion 12

ABUNDANT COURAGE

For you were called to freedom, brothers. Only do not use your freedom as an opportunity for the flesh, but through love serve one another.

GALATIANS 5:13 ESV

That cross I'd penned onto my wrist the day before, it's about rubbed off. I've got no bloody idea at all how you take this dare. How can all the bad brokenness be broken with good brokenness? How do you live cruciform—and be broken and given into a kind of communion?

There's a mama round the corner from the farm, they say she's been up for days rocking that brand-new daughter of hers who the doctors conceded last week has a fatal disease. What in God's good name was the clock on her wall saying?

I'd sat up late the night before to write back to my friend Elizabeth. We had met nearly six years ago—two mothers with nearly a dozen kids between the two of us—commiserating over houses that seemed to manufacture chaos like it was our actual business plan. I told her I was trying to remember to put my priorities on all things unseen. Told her I was trying to slay the idol of the seen, break the idols of performance, and believe the state of my house doesn't reflect the state of my soul. And she'd confirmed it's the priorities unseen—the prayers, the relationships, the love while doing the work—that hold the meaning, the merit. And she'd leaned in and asked if we could be friends for life, and I had said, "Deal," and laughed way too loud.

I couldn't have known then that Elizabeth would turn out to be unlike any other friend I'd ever had. Who else sends courage in a box and pounds of milk chocolate that would show up at the door? Who else would reach out late at night and say, "I see you, the you behind everything you're doing, and I like you—the you that just is"? Who else lived out priorities unseen—priorities that let the people around her, me, be known? I couldn't have known then that Elizabeth would be the friend for life that my life needed in ways I hadn't expected.

Then last night, Elizabeth said hospice had just started coming to the house.

How do you end up being forty-something with hospice knocking on your front door? How can God let the world break a bit like this? How is *this* all grace? How is *this* love?

I bury my head deeper into the pillow. Rub a bit at that smudged cross on my wrist . . . and yet *it is love*. Who knows why God allows heartbreak, *but the answer must be important enough because God allows His heart to break too.*

I reach for the pen on my nightstand, the way I've reached for ink to count a thousand ways He loves me, the way ink's been the cheapest of medicines. But now, can the ink be lived, branded onto the skin? How could it leave the page and lead a way through pain? The ink would start right there on my scarred wrist, right where part of me wanted to kind of die, and not in the saving way, and somehow there is good brokenness that grows out of every scar and wound we will ever suffer. *Draw one line vertically down my wrist, right over scars.* The question of evil and suffering is answered in the breaking of God's own heart too. *Draw another line horizontally across my wrist, breaking scar lines with cross lines.* Our broken hearts always break His. It's the quantum physics of God: Your one broken heart always splits God's heart in two. You never cry alone.

And still—your brokenness can feel like a tomb you can't quite claw yourself out of. Is the most painful kind of tears the kind no one can see, the kind where your soul weeps alone? You can feel the corners and edges of you withering with the weight of scar tissue on your own soul.

The flannel sheets feel like grave clothes. How long can I refuse to move? Exhale.

Maybe air isn't all that keeps you alive. There's a cross that's helping me breathe. It's reminding me, re-forming me, and I'm so insufferably forgetful. I try to remember that grace swallowed with courage is elemental to living.

Inked cross bleeding into my arms. Swallow down His grace. What He gives is enough—abundantly enough courage to move up out of bed. *One small step for a woman, one giant, abundant leap for her sanity.*

The woman with broken kids, the friend with dying friends, the ache of a broken heart. Just take the first step. And then the next step.

Courage is always reaching out and taking just a bit of that iron-nail grace.

FOR REFLECTION

- ✧ You may not know why God allows heartbreak, but the answer must be important because God allows His heart to break too. How does this change your perspective on your own brokenness?
- ✧ How are you experiencing the cruciform grace of Jesus as more than abundantly enough for your brokenness right now?

Devotion 13

MASTERING THE DARK

The light shines in the darkness, and the darkness has not overcome it.

JOHN 1:5

The old coot ran in his boots. Weren't too many of anybody who believed he could.

The kids and I read about the old guy one night after supper and the dishwasher's moaning away, crumbs still across the counter. How there's this old guy who ran 544 miles. His name was Cliff Young, and he wasn't really so so young: he was sixty-one years old. He was a farmer.[11] Levi grins big.

Mr. Young showed up for the race in his OshKosh overalls and with his work boots on, galoshes over top. Just in case it rained.

He had no Nike sponsorship. He had no wife—hadn't had one ever. Lived with his mother. Never drank. Never ran in any kind of race before. Never ran a marathon, or a half marathon, not even a five-mile race.

But here he was, standing in his work boots at the starting line of an ultramarathon, the most grueling race in the world: *544 miles.*

Try wrapping your head around pounding the concrete with one foot after another for 544 endless, stretching miles. They don't measure races like that in yards—but in zip codes.

First thing Cliff did was take out his teeth. Said his false teeth rattled when he ran. Said he grew up on a farm with sheep and no four-wheelers, no horses, so the only way to round up sheep was on the run. Sometimes the best training for the really big things is just the everyday things.

That's what Cliff said. "Whenever the storms would roll in, I'd have to go run and round up the sheep." Two thousand head of sheep. Two thousand acres of land. "Sometimes I'd have to run those sheep for two or three days. I can run this race; it's only two more days. Five days. I've run sheep for three."

"Got any backers?" Reporters shoved their microphones around old Cliff like a spike belt.

"No . . ." Cliff slipped his hands into his overall pockets.

"Then you can't run."

Cliff looked down at his boots. Does a man need backers, or does a man need to believe? What you believe is the biggest backer you'll ever have.

The other runners, all under a buffed thirty years of age, they take off like pumped shots from that starting line. And scruffy old Cliff staggers forward. He doesn't run. Shuffles, more like it. Straight back. Arms dangling. Feet awkwardly shuffling along.

Cliff eats dust. For eighteen hours, the racers blow down the road, far down the road, and old Cliff shuffles on behind. Come the pitch black of night, the runners in their $400 ergonomic Nikes and Adidas lie down by the roadside, because that's the plan to win an ultramarathon, to run 544 straight miles: 18 hours of running, 6 hours of sleeping, rise and repeat for 5 days, 6 days, 7 days. The dark falls in. Runners sleep. Cameras get turned off. Reporters go to bed.

And through the black night, one sixty-one-year-old man far behind keeps shuffling on. And all I can think is: the light shines in the darkness and the darkness has not overcome it. The light shineth in the darkness, but the darkness *comprehendeth* it not. *Katalambano*. Comprehend. Understand. Master.

Cliff Young runs on through the night, and there is an Abundant Light that shines in the darkness and the darkness *does not master it*. The darkness doesn't understand the light, doesn't comprehend the light, doesn't get the light, doesn't overcome the light, doesn't *master* the light. Darkness doesn't have anything on light, on hope, on faith.

The darkness that sucks at the prodigal kid doesn't have anything on the light of his mother's prayers. The black of pornography that threatens at the edges doesn't master the blazing light of Jesus at the center. The pit of depression that plunges deep doesn't go deeper than the love of your Jesus, and there is no place His light won't go to find you, to save you, to *hold* you. That low-lying storm cloud that hangs over you can't master the light of Christ that raises you.

"Darkness cannot drive out darkness; only light can do that."[12] Martin Luther King Jr. had said it, had lived it. Only words of Light can drive out worlds of dark. Only lives of Light can drive out lies of dark.

Darkness can never travel as fast as Light. No matter how bad things get, no matter how black the dark seeps in, no matter the depths of the night—*the dark can never travel as fast as Light.* The Light is always there first, waiting to shatter the dark.

Cliff Young runs on through the dark—because he didn't know you were supposed to stop. The accepted way professional runners approached the race was to run eighteen hours, sleep six, for seven days straight. But Cliff Young didn't know the accepted way. He only knew what he did back home, the way he had always done it: *you run through the dark.*

Turns out when Cliff Young said he gathered sheep around his farm for three days, he meant he'd run across two thousand acres of farmland for three days straight without stopping. You gathered sheep by running through the dark. So along the endless stretches of highway, Cliff gained ground because he ran *through* the dark.

For five days, fifteen hours, and four minutes straight, Cliff Young ran, never once stopping for the dark, never stopping until the old sheep farmer crossed the finish line—first—beating a world record by *two days.*

The second-place runner crossed the finish line almost *ten hours after* old Cliff.

And when they handed Mr. Young his $10,000 prize, he said he hadn't known there was a prize. Said he'd run for the wonder of it. Said that the other runners had worked hard too, so he waited at the finish line and handed each of the five who finished an equal share of the prize.

And then the old coot in boots walked away without a penny for the race but with the hearts of the world. While others run fast, you can just shuffle with perseverance. While others set out to impress, you can simply press on. While others stop for the dark, you can run *through* the dark.

When those reporters asked him afterward what kept him running through the nights, Cliff said, "I imagined I was outrunning a storm to gather up my sheep."

I sit there in the thickening dark, with the One who *mastered* the dark and *overcame* the storm to gather His sheep, and I remember that now there is one who is Abundant Light, who shines in the darkness and the darkness can *never overcome Him.*

And you can see them out the front window, far away to the west, out there on the highway, the lights all breaking through the dark.

FOR REFLECTION

- ✦ What brokenness and darkness is your marathon right now—and how can you leave it with Light Himself today?
- ✦ What would your life look like if you daily ran your race knowing that Abundant Light will never let the darkness overcome you?

ABUNDANT TIME

[Love] always protects, always trusts, always hopes, always perseveres.

1 CORINTHIANS 13:7

I had always thought of time as this highway robber that *steals* life, until we ultimately die. But the perspective of Jesus, all through the Gospels, offers a radically different perspective. Jesus speaks of time as the *highway* by which we have come to die—so we can ultimately *get to* more abundant life. Time isn't something you seize; it's something you sacrifice. It's not something to grab; it's something to *give*.

If *eucharisteo*, giving thanks, slows down time . . . then can being broken and given in communion break time by actually multiplying it? Maybe time gets broken and multiplied and made into something more whenever someone breaks and gives herself or himself away.

Death stops time for us here and makes us a seed to be buried in the ground—but maybe when we die to self, we break time here and our sacrificial love breaks into eternity, going on forever. "Love never dies."[13] Isn't that exactly what Jesus did to break time's death grip on us? He died, and His death broke a hole in the wall of time and incarnates how a cruciform abundant life is the new door for all of us to escape out of time.

Maybe temporary time is made for dying to self—so your eternal self can really live.

Have the hands of the clock stopped moving there in the kitchen? It takes courage to listen with our whole heart to the tick of God's timing rather than march to the loud beat of our fears.

Time can't dictate dreams or hijack hope or determine destination. It can't force us into living anything but what we believe. No matter what the hands of the clock say, underneath us all are the everlasting arms, and time's arms are too weak to rob any hope, steal any prayers, destroy any joy, or crush any purpose. Time never heals wounds like God does.

It's God's hands that control the universe. The hands of the clock are bound by the decisions of our hands. And He has made our hands free to be His.

I pick up a jar of wheat off the windowsill, try to count grains, envision each of those kernels as days, the only time I have. It's a *jarring* thought. *The way to break time's hold on me is to be broken and given with my time.*

There is a stray kernel on the counter, another left in the measuring cup. I pick up each gold nugget with the tip of my finger. *You can't waste one.* You can't afford not to break each grain day—*die to self*—and have twice as much life. *Wasn't the cross on my wrist daring just that?*

The shape of multiplied time looks like a cross. Cruciform. Broken and given, reaching right out.

There's enough time yet for picking glads in muggy August morning sunshine and filling Mason jar vases of blooms for sidelined, forgotten people. There's time for lingering over cups of coffee and listening to the pouring out of someone's cracked heart, time for long phone calls and shared pie and going the extra mile. And there's time to be broken and given into all the world's brokenness, because this is how to break time's hold.

At the beginning of the year, I'd left the lid off the jar of wheat, watched Shalom run her hand again and again through the kernels.

Maybe what matters isn't what we want from the time we have to live . . . but what time wants from us.

FOR REFLECTION

✧ Where is your use of time causing more brokenness than abundance?

✧ Where in your life might you die to self and live more sacrificially with your time so that you might abundantly multiply meaningful joy?

Devotion 15

ABUNDANT BRAVERY

So do not fear, for I am with you;
do not be dismayed, for I am your God.
I will strengthen you and help you;
I will uphold you with my righteous right hand.

ISAIAH 41:10

Dear Fears,
   My grandmother used to say when I started to feel a bit undone, the way she had a saying for everything: *Feed a cold, starve a fever.* So I'm giving notice here to all you nagging fears. This is the plan: when the world starts feeling a bit undone, I will feed my faith, starve my fears.

You can count on it, right about now: I'm feeding my faith in the Maker of all people, feeding faith in hope and mercy and the Slayer of giants, feeding faith in redemption and making resurrection my refrain. I'm gorging on grace and feasting on the glory of God in the moment, the sky like this, and the air in the lungs like this, and heart thrumming alive in my ears like this.

I'm grabbing all you fears by the jugular because I know you are my everyday enemy. You fears are too often my cancer, my addiction, my hidden habit. You're my jailer, my poison, my daily blade of self-harm. You've been my anesthetic, the thing I've let come freeze me every day, lock me up, and suck away my life. You've snuffed out my soul while you

68

kept on breathing for years. You're the most common brain tumor, always beginning in our minds.

You fears may think you can divide us and conquer us and imprison us in small places, in small lives, with high fences that keep out hope and possibility and each other and the lives we really want. But you don't know how we're seeing things.

You may think you can make us cynical about dreams and apathetic about hope and dubious about possibility and people and prospects. But we're all over you: you aren't meant to drive our lives; you're meant to teach us something about life. You're a chameleon that wears a thousand different masks, and there are ways to see the realest, truest, surest things.

You can sound loud and look like anger, or you can strut about and rant like pride. You can grow deathly quiet and look like numbness or apathy or indifference or a dream running in the wrong direction.

But the thing is: When I find my fears, I find my idols. When I find where you lurk, I will look you in the eye until I know your realest name. And I will say your name out loud.

Every fear is a mask for an idol. Sit long enough in the quiet and let the fear get close enough—what seems like your worst nightmare—and then let your hand flash out like a fireball of fierce redemption, rip that flimsy mask off, and name the fear for what it is.

Break your idols and you break free of all your fears.

So I will go on crushing all of your life-absorbing fears to a fine powder because this is the deal: I want to be better at letting go of you than letting go of joy. I don't have to worry about what's up ahead because Christ is the head of everything. And I don't have to fear what's around the next corner because Christ is already there too.

We don't have to abide in our fears because we can abide in our Father.

There's believing it and then there's abundantly living it: Fear is a liar, and love hands out keys. Love is infinite and love can't ever end, and if love doesn't ever run out, what is there ever to fear? There will still be love when the worst happens and when the hope doesn't happen. There will still be love when everything's crumbling, and there will be enough love to rebuild. There will still be enough love to keep breathing, to keep believing, to keep being and being brave.

For this I know: Fear can be what we feel, but brave is what we do. And there's enough brave in me to believe that though the world is broken, there is light getting in . . . That though the busted road ahead may head through the dark, there is more than abundantly enough love around every bend that will carry more than I can imagine . . . That though there may be battles ahead to brave, as long as I keep holding on to love, there is never any losing.

It's strange how that is, how hate is never the enemy like fear actually is. And every fear shatters, breaks away, when it turns to face the relentless, abundant love that will not be stopped by anything.

FOR REFLECTION

- ✧ What fears in your life might be idols that need to be broken?
- ✧ How are you abundantly feeding your faith? And daily starving your fears?

Devotion 16

GROWING ABUNDANCE

For we know in part and we prophesy in part, but when completeness comes, what is in part disappears.

1 CORINTHIANS 13:9–10

It's been a late spring. Cold and wet. As if the sun's been hiding, grieving a loud and polarized world.

When the sky finally leaks itself dry, the Farmer and one of his freckled girls head to the barren fields with their seeds and their willing hands. The Farmer wears the sweatshirt he's had since before she was born. She wears a smile a mile wide.

You can relax into an easy smile when you trust that your father holds your world.

The girl's never broken the earth before. So he walks across the field to show her how to run the cultivator, how to make a seedbed in front of him with the planter. How to break up the soil. He shows her how to shift and run the hydraulic levers, when to lift, drop, and turn to coordinate the whole dance. She never takes her eyes off him, nodding, repeating, memorizing.

A field has to be broken open before it can grow anything.

And he says what he always says: "Just stay steady. No fits and starts—just stay steady. Trust it as it comes." I hear too . . . nod too.

Steadiness is a balm to brokenness.

I say what I always say, maybe for me the most: "Don't be afraid. Don't even be afraid of being afraid."

And she winks. "Got it."

Spring's warming on our shoulders. You can feel fear but you don't have to be afraid of being afraid. When you aren't afraid of being afraid, you transform fear into friend. They break that ground like breaking open a piñata, and the breaking can make you believe in good things coming.

Sure, she may be intimidated by the tractor, but the thing is—feelings can accompany you, but they don't get to control you. Feelings get to inform you, but they don't get to form you. Feelings get to keep you company, but they don't get to keep you in bondage. Only God keeps you.

The girl breaks the field, again and again. The field smells earthy, like loamy possibility. And brokenness never has to be the end—brokenness can be the beginning of growth.

The only way for anything to grow—is for something to break. Growth only happens when the status quo is broken. Change can only happen when what is—is broken. Do not be afraid of broken things; this is the beginning of changing things, of growing things.

Our girl pulls down the field, breaking open the earth so that seeds can break in the darkest places and then resurrect to abundant life. And I sit on the edge of the field and watch.

There's that cross drawn this morning on my wrist. *What looks more broken than the cross? But what wins more than the cross?*

The cross doesn't look like it's winning. More like it's losing, pouring out, being given—to those who don't love at all. It conquers everything, but it looks more broken than anything. Jesus' cross proves it: Love may not seem self-fulfilling, but in actual fact, deepest love looks deeply broken. His cross nailed it down: Love wins when it looks broken. Broken and given and poured out.

You have to learn how to suffer like Christ, because this is love. Tell the newlyweds, the new parents, the world: When you are most loving, suffering will most likely result. Doing the right thing may not look like success but suffering—and that may be the most successful of all.

This isn't sexy or trendy. Nobody's hawking this on social media or the shelves of Target, and my heart breaks for that a bit. Watching the breaking up of the earth down the expanse of field, the thought comes: *Is God's definition of love about breaking our happiness—or breaking us free from the self-love that threatens to imprison us all?*

Maybe this is the question that can reshape our world.

God's love doesn't translate into fulfilling my desires. God is love. That doesn't mean self-fulfillment. "God is love" means to deny self. It means accepting suffering and being broken open and poured out.

Love doesn't win if you're only loving yourself. We can forget: God may not affirm our desires, but He will firmly nail those desires to the cross and affirm the rising of Christ through those desires. And the beauty of Christianity is—*what dies will rise.* When you're called to a cross, God is always calling us to our greatest good—and to a greater abundance.

The wind blows across the field behind one girl who is being brave behind the wheel. *There are truths that will change the world because they never change.* The girl looks to her father and catches his eye and smiles. She trusts her father to plant what will rise, and this is the beauty of brave.

Walking back across the field to the pickup parked at the road, the open and willing ground crumbles under my steps. And I can't help but ache a bit with the surrendered beauty of it here, just as it comes.

Only a broken field yields.

✧ If growth only happens when the status quo is broken, why might you be afraid of broken things? Where are you praying for change? What might God need to break for growth to happen in that area? How is God calling you to surrender today?

✧ When you are most loving, suffering will most likely result. How does that change your expectations of what an abundant life looks like? Reflect on whether God's definition of love truly breaks you free from the self-love that threatens to imprison you.

LIVING GIVENNESS

Humble yourselves before the Lord, and he will lift you up.

JAMES 4:10

The best way to de-stress is to bless.

Slipping up behind Hope, both arms around her shoulders, I pull the girl in close, kiss her on the top of her head. "You? Looks like you could use a hug."

"Mummy." She turns, thinly half smiles, tilts her head into mine, and I rest my cheek on her hair.

I don't know how to love like I want. I don't know how to smooth out angst or stress or worry, but I know you either leave your worries with God . . . or your worries will make you leave God.

Honestly, I don't know how to be what she needs me to be, or what anyone needs me to be. I don't know how to become cruciform. But maybe life isn't overwhelming when we simply understand how to give, just in this moment. I don't know—maybe all there is to living, to loving, is to live into the givenness of the moment. She looks like she just needs arms to hold her. "Attention is the rarest and purest form of generosity," is what Simone Weil said.[14]

"You're kind of scared about everything you've got ahead of you?" I say it into her hair quietly.

She nods, and I pull her closer, and she's so much like me and what if she ends up taking my ways of quiet desperation and I have no idea if I'm doing anything right and *what in the world am I so afraid of?* I can see the laundry on the line in the orchard, giving itself to the wind, pockets turned out and surrendered.

And I can feel Hope breathing slow, feel my stress ebb, feel it in the warmth between us. We all long for the belonging of communion, and yet there's this fear of the closeness of the fellowship. Love is our deepest longing— and what we most deeply fear. Love breaks us vulnerably open—and then can break us with rejection. There's this craving for genuine communion—and yet this fear of losing genuine independence. Need can be a terrifying thing. I know—I've built my fair share of fortress walls. You can crave communion but fear being used or manipulated or smothered or burned. I have used a thousand buckets to douse any spark of a terrifying, vulnerable communion.

How can I keep forgetting? Write it up my arms: *koinonia* is always, always the miracle.

"We're here, and we're for you." I whisper it, press the words into a gentle kiss on her forehead, and maybe there's a bit of *koinonia* in the stress. Maybe the cross penned on my wrist is pressing the possibility of new ways of meaning and being and transforming right into the bone of things.

"There are very few men who realize what God would make of them if they abandoned themselves entirely to His hands, and let themselves be formed by His Grace," wrote Ignatius.[15]

What would happen if the abandoned abandoned themselves into His heart and let themselves be formed by His cross?

FOR REFLECTION

- ✧ How are you letting *koinonia* and love break you free to experience a meaningful, vulnerable communion?
- ✧ How might you abandon yourself to the abundance of His heart and let yourself be formed by His cross?

HEART TRANSPLANT

Many waters cannot quench love;
rivers cannot sweep it away.

SONG OF SONGS 8:7

They don't tell you this: that love is only known by the fools. You just feel it sometimes, the ache of love, of all the things, right there underneath your breastbone.

The end of spring, I watch a ninety-two-year-old man lean over a casket and hold his face in his gnarled, wrinkly hands and weep over the stiff, frail body of his wife. I can't turn my eyes away from his hands.

He'd brought her dinner the last several years, washed her hair with those hands, turned back her sheets, and spooned close to her every night for a span of seventy years. When they soundlessly roll her casket out of the church, his son pushes his creaking wheelchair behind her in that oak box.

And the old man bends into this sobbing grief that fills the sanctuary, and all the farmers in their uncomfortable ties and all us farmers' wives in our pressed black skirts, we bow our heads and listen to his unashamed grief. This is the sound of a fool who gave his heart away to one woman for a stretch of seventy-two vowed years.

Is this what a heart transplant feels like, when a lifetime of love turns out to give your heart to someone else? There wasn't one of us standing there yesterday who didn't know it: *his heart's inside that casket, inside of her.*

It's God who gives us our first heart transplant, who gives us a heart of flesh, and then we keep giving our hearts away, bits of us transplanted out of our aloneness and into the hollow spaces of others.

Not one of us said it then, that love is for the fools and the givers, for the pourers who tip their hearts right over, for the riskers who lay their whole hearts down on tables without a wall or a shield in sight and feel afraid but give their vulnerable heart anyway.

The end of March, right after I left Mrs. Bender's funeral, right after I feel in my chest the ache of Mr. Bender's heart transplant, I stop, just before April shows up on the first with all her foolishness, and I watch a man say good-bye to his girl at the airport, watch how she buries her head into his offered shoulder, how he strokes back her hair, how she mouths into his neck, "I don't want to go."

He'd walked her to class, given her his coat, his arm, a necklace, the shirt off his own back, bits of his heart. She'd given him a ready smile, an always listening ear, always the meeting of her eyes.

And there, before she steps into that airport security line, his arm around her waist pulls her in and he looks down at the floor, looks for words, tries to fight back his heart giving way all liquid: *"You . . . just . . . just—I have no other place to go. You are my heart. You are my home."*

He can't stop his chin from trembling. Our heart's true home is never inside of us but inside of someone else.

Inside of Him, inside of people.

We are always lost until our heart makes its home inside of someone else. Our lives are unfulfilling if we only let our hearts fill us instead of filling other people's broken places. The art of living is believing there is enough love in you, that you are loved enough by Him, to be made into love to give.

Fulfilling lives happen when we give our hearts to fill other people's empty spaces.

When he said to her, "You—you are my heart. You are my home"—she

78

looked up at him, looked him in the eye, and her heart leaked down her cheek in this singular gleaming tear.

After they drive away with Mrs. Bender's casket with Mr. Bender's heart transplanted into her after seventy years of loving her, after the planes fly with hearts, hearts making their home outside of the wavers and the weepers, I stop in the early evening in a doorway, watch our youngest boy who's diabetic sleeping deep on the couch. In too deep a sleep. We shake his shoulders but he won't wake, won't open his eyes.

"Test his blood." I murmur the words, gently nudging the pale white boy, his sister looking for his blood tester. Another sister runs to the barn, calls for the Farmer to come.

When we prick his finger, press the tip for drops of blood, dip a test strip into the pooling scarlet, there's a circle of us waiting for the number to pop up on the tester's screen, to tell us what runs through the veins of our diabetic boy.

The startlingly low number that shocks the screen in his sister's hand sends us all into a desperate whirl. A brother lifts the boy, a sister wipes off the beading sweat, the Farmer gets him to open his mouth, and we try to get him to drink juice, to eat an emergency roll of candy, before he slips into a hypoglycemic coma.

And I look around at us. *This is us.* Us given to each other. The heart's true home is addressing the brokenness of other hearts.

When the boy starts to come to, his dad, still in barn clothes, sits with him, steadying hand on his shoulder, eyes reassuring his boy, waiting for color to return to the boy's cheeks. His older sister gathers up his diabetic supplies, returns everything to his bag. His brother heads back out to the barn and birthing sows and all our unfinished chores.

I scoop up the baby, change her sagging diaper, smooth back her black hair, cup her grinning face, plant a row of kisses across her forehead. Answer a text from our oldest son who couldn't find a bed in a hostel last night in Florence so he pulled on every piece of clothing he had in his backpack and slept on the cold street outside the locked airport, waiting for his 6:30 a.m. flight out.

This is us being stretched thin, and our lives become thin places to see the hand of God. And when our hearts find their home outside of ourselves, our hearts rest in Him.

Yes, sure, they tell you that love is a choice. They go around telling you that love is a verb. But no one tells you exactly what verb that precisely is.

You could look around you and think love is a verb and maybe that looks like love wants, love controls, love demands, love keeps score, love self-focuses, love manipulates, love self-protects. Someone should tell us exactly what verb love is. Love is a verb, and that verb is *give*. Love gives.

God is love and He gets to define love: "For God so loved the world *that he gave . . .*"[16] That's what love is: Love gives. There is no other way to express love apart from givenness. The essence of love is living given. Give away your life; you'll find life given back, but not merely given back—given back with bonus and blessing. Giving, not getting, is the way.

Love gives. Love gives its life for another life. This is the definitive proof of love. Love is not that we get to feel something, but that we give ourselves to someone. The end of March, I stop, before April walks in with everyone acting like fools at the beginning, I stop and am hushed by Christ carrying the cross. Love always reaches out. So if love isn't shaped like a cross, it isn't really love. Love self-gives, not self-focuses.

Mr. Bender had loved her, and a casket would never change that. Give away your heart and you transplant your heart into eternity. The Farmer helps our boy with diabetes to his feet. I witness how the son looks over at his dad, how his dad smiles. A plane is flying through night, into the sun, one man's heart at home in his lady.

And at the end of every single day, my friend, Mei, she, without fail, asks me two questions that answer the meaning to being, to everything, two questions that are forming my heart: *How did you give thanks today? And how did you live given?*

Love is a verb, and that verb is *give*. And the most powerful word in the world is *given* and love gives thanks and love lives given. I know no other way to the abundant life . . . because this is the only way Jesus lived. Only the life that is given gives any joy. Only the life that is surrendered wins joy. Only the life that you lose wins the meaningful life you want to find.

At the end of spring, I stop and read that there's a comet that will fall across the sky on April Fools' Day, making its closest pass to earth ever on record. This one blazing comet will fall close over our farm boy with his bag full of insulin needles, will fall over Mr. Bender hunched over the memories of Mrs. Bender carrying his transplanted heart into eternity, over a plane winging toward the dawn of home and open arms. And all the loving fools could look up to the heavens and see this comet of light, this light given.

And there it is, beating at the heart of the universe, beating like a steadying rhythm in all of us: *live given, live given, live given.*

FOR REFLECTION

✧ Where is your broken heart most at home?

✧ What could possibly change in your life by asking yourself every day: *What have I been given that I can give thanks for? And because I have been given so much, how am I living given?*

Devotion 19

YIELDING INTO
GIVENNESS

*The Son of Man did not come to be served, but to serve, and
to give his life as a ransom for many.*

MATTHEW 20:28

The light feels warm. Dappled on faces. The Farmer, Hope and Shalom between us, only nods to me. There's not much to say when you feel a holy change beginning: Our broken night could become like the noonday. Light could rise in all this darkness—in us, in the ache of unspoken broken, in all this busted world. We will begin here and trust that this will lead us: spending yourself is how you pay attention to joy; spending yourself is how you *multiply joy.*

The angling sun sends shafts of light between the trees and onto us all standing there, and over the heads of father and daughters, I can see how this myriad of insects had webbed their way in the beams, ascending and descending like glory bits from seraphs' wings. *I was made for this. The universe was made for giving. Givenness.*

"Every Christian," wrote C. S. Lewis, "is to become a little Christ. The whole purpose of becoming a Christian is simply nothing else . . . It is even doubtful, you know, whether the whole universe was created for any other purpose."[17]

We exist to be Little Christs. Not Little Ladder Climbers. Not Little Control Freaks. Not Little Convenience Dwellers. Simply little giving Christs. Not ever in a way that's divine, but simply, always, and in every way, disciples.

The term *Christian* means exactly that—"little Christ" . . . and that ending in the original Greek—*ianos*—it means to be patterned after something. The cross on my wrist—I am beginning to feel the pattern, the form, of everything. Dietrich Bonhoeffer's words reverberate: "When Christ calls a man, He bids him come and die."[18] And Lewis leans in: "Christ says 'Give Me All. I don't want so much of your time and so much of your money and so much of your work: I want you. I have not come to torment your natural self, but to kill it.'"[19]

Come die. In a thousand ways. "Give Me all. I want you. I want you all." Give not only all my best, but even all my brokenness?

Watching the light with the Farmer and our daughters under the canopy of maples, I remembered Lewis's words echoing Christ: "I don't want to cut off a branch here and a branch there, I want to have the whole tree down . . . Hand over the whole natural self, all the desires which you think innocent as well as the ones you think wicked—the whole outfit. I will give you a new self instead. In fact, I will give you Myself: my own will shall become yours."[20]

It's like an echo of communion, of that intimate exchange of the givenness in my brokenness and the givenness of His acceptance. "All His is mine and all mine is His." *My own will shall become yours.* "Both harder and easier than what we are all trying to do."[21] It's like Lewis knows what I'm thinking.

You have noticed, I expect, that Christ Himself sometimes describes the Christian way as very hard, sometimes as very easy. He says, "Take up your Cross"—in other words, it is like going to be beaten to death in a concentration camp. Next minute He says, "My yoke is easy and my burden light." He means both . . . The terrible thing, the almost impossible thing, is to hand over your whole self—all your wishes and precautions—to Christ. But it is far easier than what we are all trying to do instead. For what we are trying to do is to remain what we call "ourselves," to keep personal happiness as our great aim in life, and yet at the same time be "good" . . . If I want to produce wheat, the change must go deeper than the surface. I must be ploughed up and re-sown.[22]

Hand over your whole self. Your whole broken self. *Givenness*. Because this is far easier than pretending to be whole and not broken.

There is a strange sense of surrender happening, a surrender in all things. The heart has to be broken and plowed and re-sown if it's going to yield. The change must go deeper than the surface. This is only the beginning. There's a bucket of wheat at the back door—time—and there's enough given to you to satisfy your soul—everything you need.

And if you want your life to yield, there has to be a yielding in the soul. There is a plowing that breaks your soul to grow you.

Under the trees I reach over and find Hope's hand.

"A good day, Mama, a good birthday day." She swings my hand high like those kids at the park. Her smile feels like grace.

"Nah." The Farmer grins, Shalom swinging from his arm. "A *great* day. The best day."

FOR REFLECTION

❖ How are you handing over your whole self—your whole broken self—in givenness?

❖ How are you spending yourself to pay attention to joy? Because how you're spending yourself is how you *multiply abundant joy*.

Devotion 20

HOLY HAPPINESS

Submit yourselves, then, to God. Resist the devil, and he will flee from you.

JAMES 4:7

I was once tempted beyond measure. *And c'mon, we've all been tempted beyond measure countless times.*

It was a temptation that wooed my wounds, curled around me in the dark like tender comfort that ended up cutting off shavings of my heart. It consumed my thoughts as if it could slurp down my resolve like a slushy in a heat wave south of the Mason-Dixon Line.

There are temptations that can feel more like completions. I let my dreams wander like a lost bird winging and circling for its own kind of home. You can feel as though if you just give into what you want, you'll be given the abundant joy you've always wanted.

That's the popular tripe on the streets these days, and I confess I once nearly bought that prepackaged little sound bite of pop psychology— *because it didn't come with any warning that it would also gut your life.*

I didn't know until my heart almost bled itself dry that there are really only two choices when begging temptation looks you square in your twitching eye: there is either the pain of self-denial, or the pain of self-destruction.

I think about that a lot now when temptation beckons me with the lie:

85

"Take, eat, and see that the comfort is good." *Pain of self-denial, or pain of self-destruction.* Heaven is forever, and here is a blink, and narrow is The Way to joy.

They'll tell you there's no such thing called temptation anymore, only repressed self-limitation. They'll tell you temptation isn't an issue for the sophisticated. And I want to say: just don't say you're a follower of Christ if you're actually following your own heart.

Someone once told me she'd found courage to follow her heart's desires. I watched light move across her like clouds across the fields, and I loved her. But love doesn't mean agreement. Love means sacrifice. And I didn't have words then. I learned them through my own bloody battles, and I ask them, limping: Do we follow our heart's desires—or do we desire to follow Christ? Courage isn't doing what you want in life; courage is *laying down your life.* Otherwise it's not courage—it's self-gratification.

Courage is always selfless: *less self, which ultimately means more holy happiness for your soul.*

These aren't mere words; they are divine lifelines that have made me weep for the cost of them. I wanted to cup her face, ask if we could try to find brave together where two rugged beams intersect and Real Love could show us how to feel holy joy. Because I knew those who seek to be happy must first seek to be holy. *And there is no true happiness apart from true holiness.*

If you want to be popular and please people, you might believe your life must preach happiness. But if you want to profoundly please God, you must make your life *preach holiness.* "Holiness, not happiness, is the chief end of man," urged Oswald Chambers.[23] Because holiness is not a single attribute of God—*but a synonym for all of who God is.*

He is love—but His love is a holy love, His grace is a holy grace, His justice is holy justice, and His spirit is Holy Spirit. And the call to holiness is a trinity of its own: "separation from sin, dedication to God, transformation into Christ's image."[24]

This is hard—*but we do hard and holy things*. So don't trust any author's words about happiness or holiness unless you've opened the Word and know they line up with what the Author of the universe says.

I lay awake in the dark after I was once tempted beyond measure. And it turns out nothing kills temptation or self-loathing like the freedom of already being crucified with Christ. I traced it with a fingertip, that cross I pen every day on my wrist the way a child writes on her hand what she must remember, what she can't afford to ever forget. All that we're tempted to do or all that we're tempted to self-loathe has already been nailed to the cross.

This is the love story I never want to get over: The things we wish we could change about ourselves have already been exchanged at the cross. When we need radical change, we need only to look to where radical exchange has already happened—at the cross. Cruciformation is the essence of transformation because it's at the cross where radical change happens—our brokenness is exchanged for His wholeness. This is what gives courage. This is what destroys temptations. Whisper *cruciform*, and in that moment you're dead to all the brokenness that keeps you from breaking free. Whisper *cruciform*, and you're dead to addictions and wrong ambitions and ugly sedition. Whisper *cruciform*, and you're dead to what wants to kill and destroy you.

Only to the extent that we let ourselves die over and over again can the abundant life be found in us. Only to the extent that we let ourselves be formed cruciform over and over again can our lives be fully transformed. This is what transforms everything.

The mind is renewed in Christ when the mind returns to the cross-wounds, the words, the ways, the wooing of Christ.

This is holy happiness. What frees you to fully live is letting yourself be fully crucified with Christ. Love wins only when it's givenness, not selfishness. Otherwise *it's not love*. *Cruciform* is the form of anything that wins. Ask Jesus. *Cruciform is the form of my new identity, the form of my never-failing security, the form of my needed serenity.*

Don't let anyone tell you different. Jesus says, "Don't run from suffering; embrace it. Follow me and I'll show you how. Self-help is no help at all. Self-sacrifice is the way, my way, to saving yourself, your true self."[25]

Embrace the cross-life so you can have the abundant life.

Preaching cruciform to yourself is what transforms your soul—your world, your joy.

I was once tempted beyond measure—and I felt it in the dark, how He stretched out one arm and then the other, and the universe reverberated with the cry:

Look at My outstretched arms. I love you beyond measure. And My arms, My Way, My Love, is more than abundantly enough.

Jesus is abundantly enough. This is the love story that woos your wounds, that binds your broken heart to His, that heals the aching hurt of all the unspoken broken.

There is a Way bigger than your wants. You can never miss out on holy happiness for all eternity. Jesus is abundantly more fulfilling than anything that you want. Your Jesus wants you, and don't you want to be abundantly wanted the most?

I once watched a bird unfold its wings and give itself to the wind. And when it took to the sky, outstretched, a cross-formed shadow moved like grace across our fields and beyond the narrow gate.

You could see it: its joy knew no bounds or measurement as it soared toward those holy heights.

FOR REFLECTION

✧ In what ways are you being tempted right now toward brokenness and away from the abundant life? How are you fighting through that temptation so you can fully experience the abundant life?

✧ What if every time you experienced temptation this week, you whispered *cruciform*? What if you drew a cross daily on your wrist and you intentionally made that one word, *cruciform*, the beat of your heart, the repeating refrain of your thoughts? Would you dare to whisper it as the password into the abundant life?

Part Three

How Do You Let Your Broken Heart Receive?

UNASHAMED BROKENNESS

*So do not be ashamed of the testimony about our Lord or
of me his prisoner. Rather, join with me in suffering for the
gospel, by the power of God.*

2 TIMOTHY 1:8

I get to lie right next to our baby girl every night. Sometimes we have to
pull close, to loan each other courage to reach through the dark and
find what we need. Rubbing her back in these small, slow circles feels like
polishing down the day to the essence of grace.

She reaches up her little hand. *"Mama? Back? Back?"* And as I rub
her back, she rests her hand on my back.

Her tiny palm slides back and forth across the small of my back—like
grace given always comes back to find you, hold you.

She feels like hushed holiness in the dark, and I don't move.

She'd come terrified and heartbroken to us, ten thousand kilometers
across the world, and her eyes were so wide, like if she looked hard enough,
enlarged herself enough, she would find a safe place.

For months I've rocked and held and stayed closest, and she and I,
we've bonded into a kind of courage. And now she rubs my back in the
dark and I rub hers and I memorize this: safe places are your very own
miracles that hand you comfort in one hand and courage in the other.

Her hand rests on me and mine on hers.

"*Mama? Mama?*" She pats my arm. And when I look up, she takes her hand and pulls up her shirt and runs her fingers up and down the raised purpling scar that splits her chest.

"Brave."

She says the word in the dark. She says it over and over again.

She's tracing her scar.

"Brave. Brave."

I've always called the evidence of her open-heart surgery her *brave scar* . . . but she's just calling it? Her *brave*.

Yes, Brokenhearted—your scar is proof of your brave.

And you don't have to be ashamed of it, you don't have to hide it, you don't have to pretend it doesn't exist. You can pull back your shirt any time and show me, a hundred times a day; you can take my hand and ask me to trace your brave. Because I have found this in all the dark: we are all called to be witnesses. Trust me, life testifies that this is what it's all about: *we are all called to be witnesses.*

I touch her scar and whisper it with her, witness it with her: *Brave, Brave.*

Never be ashamed, Brokenhearted, never be ashamed.

Shame dies when stories are told in safe places. *Shame poisons hope*—poisons the hope that things can change. That we can ever be changed, ever be accepted, ever be good enough.

You can trace those scars and let it feed your courage and feel no shame for the wars you've come through, no shame for any of your broken because—*shame eats souls.*

I believe it, and touching her scars, there's C. S. Lewis: "Don't you think the things people are most ashamed of are the things they can't help?"[26]

Sometimes you can't help where you're broken, you can't help how the story turned out, you can't help how things fell apart and you got banged and busted up. And shame about the things you can't help—helps you the least.

I can trace the truth of it: *Shame* of scars can *scar worse* than the original scars. *Shame* of being broken can break us worse than being broken.

And I wish it hadn't taken me so long to know, but I've felt it in the marrow of my bones: we can live with the *pain* of brokenness, but what can slay us is the *shame* of brokenness.

Maybe on the days we want out of our lives, it isn't so much that we want to *die* from shame as *hide* from shame.

She pats her scar like it's a kind of medal, a kind of memory.

Shame gets unspeakable power only if it's unspeakable.

"Brave." She says it again.

And I nod, kiss her forehead. "*Yeah—crazy brave, girl.*" I want to write it right into her scars: You know what? Your scars are proof that you're a kind of bulletproof.

Proof that He'll carry you through *anything*, get you through *everything*, so you can be stopped by *nothing*. Scars are proof that you can now weather any storm because Jesus didn't just calm one storm but all storms, and these *scars are proof that you're a kind of bulletproof* because living through the *hardest* battles proves you can live through *any battle*.

Your scars—the worst nightmares that you survive—prove you're a kind of Kevlar.

"Hug? Hug?" she whispers. Then flings both arms of hers around my neck, her chest scar pressing up against me—her brave touching me. We loan each other the courage of scars, the bravery to be.

I pull her in closer, and brave can feel like a thousand things. Scars may come, but shame never has to.

I can feel it, right next to me, her brave breaking into a flame igniting the night.

For Reflection

✧ Where have you experienced shame? Where have you been ashamed of soul scars, and how is being ashamed of those emotional scars proving to be even more deeply scarring?

✧ How might emotional scars from your past actually be telling a different story, a story of proof—that you're now a kind of bullet-proof? How might your scars be lending you abundant courage?

Devotion 22

RELENTLESS LOVE

Jesus straightened up and asked her, "Woman, where are they? Has no one condemned you?"

"No one, sir," she said.

"Then neither do I condemn you," Jesus declared. "Go now and leave your life of sin."

JOHN 8:10–11

The Farmer's faithful hands work along the arch of my feet, and I can hardly breathe. It feels incomprehensible: God gives grace and acceptance *before* we break our sin.[27] Because it's His grace and acceptance that enable you to break sin. You never have to overcome your brokenness to claim God's love. *His love has already overcome your brokenness and claimed you.*

The wondrous order of Christianity isn't "go and sin no more and Jesus won't condemn you." The order of Christ and Christianity is "neither do I condemn you—go and sin no more." This grace reorders everything in His radically gentle way. Just as God didn't give His commandments and then see if the people were worthy of freedom from captivity, Jesus frees us with His love and then captures our hearts with His new order.

It's the experience of being daily touched by His willingness to save us first that moves us to be daily broken and given ourselves. It's His beautiful, relentless love that makes our lives relentlessly beautiful, not any striving to measure up or work to follow any commandments.

The touch of my husband's hands on my feet is this tender loosening, a metaphor. A slow understanding is unfurling somewhere between my lungs and rib cage. God's declaration of "NO CONDEMNATION" is the seed of all transformation. Habits of self-condemnation can only change when they're taken to the cross of Jesus, not to the court of judgment. Go to the cross first and hear *no condemnation*; then go to the mirror and see deep transformation. There is always more grace in Christ than there is guilt in us.

There is a grace that's strong enough to cover the things I wish I hadn't done, and the good things I wish I had. The heaviest weight of condemnation can come for all those things undone.

His thumb massages around, around, across the ball of my foot. If I could let him love me, I could let Him love me. I could receive His pouring out—even for me.

I want to look him in the eye and say what I'm finding in this slow, circuitous way: everyone is always asking only one thing: *Will you love me?*

But I say nothing. And neither does he. We say what we're always saying without saying a word. We sit in the dark house, in a ring of light from one lamp. *Can those who feel unlovable bear to be loved?*

He looks up and smiles. I close my eyes, hardly bearing the tenderness.

But isn't this the way of love? Love *bears* all things?[28] "To bear," *stego* in the Greek. It literally means a thatch roof. Love is a roof.

Love bears all things like a roof bears the wind and the rain, like a roof that bears the burden of lashing storms, brutal heat. Like a bucket poured right out that could make a roof over your head to absorb storms, that gives itself as a container to carry the burdens of others.

Real love is a roof. Real love makes you into a shelter, real love makes you into a safe place. Real love makes you safe. *Stego*.

If I can learn to receive, can I become love that breaks itself open, that pours itself out and becomes a roof over another? *Stego*. No matter what they're saying, everyone's asking, "Can you just love me?"

I brave looking down at him. He's still looking up. Let him pour out. Let yourself receive. Do not be afraid of this kind of communion. *Stego*—come in and be safe.

He's cupping my heel, massaging slow, pressing it all back, making a safe shelter over me.

"You must be so tired." I hardly whisper it, not wanting to be more of a burden for him, wanting to draw my feet away but not wanting to withdraw from him. *Let the love come, be vulnerable enough to let the brokenhearted love come, and let it fill your brokenness.*

"No . . ." He smiles. "I'm not tired . . . not now."

The moment of givenness, of pouring out—of becoming a roof—it's like that: *weightless.*

FOR REFLECTION

✧ How do you need to learn to receive so you can become love that breaks itself open, that pours itself out and becomes a roof over another?

✧ Who has been *stego* for you, and who can you be *stego* to? Because becoming a safe place, a roof for someone, and experiencing *stego* when you need a safe place are essential for a meaningful, abundant life.

Devotion 23

ABUNDANTLY SAFE

One who has unreliable friends soon comes to ruin,
but there is a friend who sticks closer than a brother.

PROVERBS 18:24

I once stood in a room awash in the palest light falling tired through worn sheer curtains.

And one woman stood in front of that window, cupping her child like she was holding a part of her heart, and I could hear her singing this lullaby like it was her baby's heartbeat, like it was all the questions pounding in our broken hearts:

When I am lost, who will come and find me? When I forget who I am, who will come and remind me? When life tries to break me, who will come and remake me?

Who knew how long and loud those three questions would reverberate through my weary veins? For months, I've been there. Who knew that everything would turn around to be about those three haunting heartbeats? *Find me, remind me, remake me?*

You can love your life and your people and feel the strange, lingering ache of loneliness in your bones. And if you were crumbling a little bit every day—who would take the time to come find you and remind you? Who would stop what they're doing to come see how your heart was beating, how you were being brave to keep being? So many people just trying to get somewhere, to get something done, they don't really have time for anyone.

I have stood in rooms and been startled by this feeling that had lodged in my heart without me inviting it in, without it ever introducing itself—but there it was: It can be terrifying to feel the singular loneliness of feeling deeply unknown. You can stand in crowded, loud rooms of tinkling glasses, flowing with raucous laughter and smooth lines, and you can wonder when that feeling will end—or wonder if you have always lived with a low-grade loneliness. The poverty that's most easily forgotten but most deeply felt is the poverty of friendship.

While the winter winds blew in here the other week, I sat with a woman and a cup of steaming tea. Maybe these days we're all just looking for safe places more than ever. Maybe right now, we're all parched for safe people.

Now, I had sipped my dark Earl Grey and I had told her I was just fine and she had looked up and smiled. "It's never fine to say you're just fine. Real friendship says, *You have a safe place at the table—to lay your whole heart down on the table.*"

So I'd exhaled into her smile—and aren't we all just looking for a safe place these days?—and the words spilled:

"You know why you've become a safe place for me? Safe people let you come unmasked, unafraid, unreserved. Truly safe people let you come with your truest self—and truly accept you."

The wind's whistling around the window and the steam from the tea is rising. "That's rare. Because usually? Usually people want their own agenda—more than they want to hear your authentic heart. Usually, we want others' hearts to be a certain way, beat a certain way—so we can have our own way."

How many times have I done this? It's hard to let people's hearts just get to beat the way they are, and safely hold them as they are.

Sometimes we try to manipulate hearts to beat the way *we want* rather than letting people's hearts communicate what *they need*. It takes courage just to listen to a heart exactly as it is and not try to manipulate its beat. Sometimes it's tempting to drum our thinking into others instead of letting people march to their own drum. We get to be like Jesus to people as they march to their own drum. And it's only Jesus who gets to change drums.

It's strange how the world, your day, can feel like a minefield. I tell that to my friend. I don't tell her how there's this lump in my throat and I'm getting weary of being brave, how health needs for your children can chafe you a bit raw, how every step forward can feel like battling hurricane winds and the whole world around you can feel like it's fracturing angry and polarizing and loud.

And she whispers it to me: "*Stego*. I will always be your *stego*."

Stego—it's become my shorthand for "I'll be your safe place."

How can one word mean what we all need? *I'll be like a roof to you. I'll be like a home to you. I'll be a safe place when you feel like you have no place.*

When you need a place to go, I'll be your *stego*. When you're tired of how the winds blow, you can count on me as *stego*. When you feel like life's been whipped into a tornado, you have a place to go, because I'm *always, always, always* your *stego*.

Love bears all things because love is a roof, love is making a safe place, love is always feeling like there's a home to come into out of the winds—love is *stego*.

It comes like the quietest breath through the spruce trees standing in the ebbing snow: people have broken hearts—so accept brokenness.

The world may feel broken and the headlines may feel loud, but there are people who break the winds, who are a roof, who are *stegos* in storms.

The February winds in the orchard keep warming, the sun braving winter, growing stronger—a testament that winds and winters and ways can always change.

And the reaching limbs of the spruce trees are their own kind of *stego*—making places that break the wind.

You can see all the lost sparrows gathering there—safe.

FOR REFLECTION

✧ Whose brokenness are you being called to be *stego* for today? What would that look like?

✧ If a meaningful, abundant life is about relationship, *koinonia*, how are you a safe place who finds, reminds, remakes for broken hearts? Consider a time when you have felt lost . . . or forgotten . . . or broken. How is God your always *stego*? How has be been finding, reminding, remaking you?

Devotion 24

SACRIFICIAL GIVENNESS

This is how we know what love is: Jesus Christ laid down his life for us. And we ought to lay down our lives for our brothers and sisters.

1 JOHN 3:16

Light from the rising moon splashes across the wall, across a framed photo of our wedding day taken in the barn because it'd rained that day. We had been in need of a roof. I've never stopped being in need.

The Farmer, he'd written out a check for the hydro, the vet, the phone, today in this Bic-blue inky scrawl. I saw him sign his name, hunt for a stamp. I didn't say anything, my arms full of wet laundry for the line, tired jeans, faithful plaids.

After the sun dried them out in the grove of ash trees, after I slung Grandma Nelly's wicker basket on my hip to go unclip their warmth from the line, I found him dangling on an aluminum ladder at the corner of the house, a tool belt around his middle, working on the eave at the edge of the roof.

"What are you up to now?" It's the way he wears his work, his dirt, like he's broken out of the earth, his jeans looking like he's wrangled for a piece of this sod.

He doesn't even look down from the ladder. I hear the smile in his words: "Loving you."

Two words, and he'd stopped my heart: *loving you.* Every to-do list can be a to-love list.

I stood there looking up at him on top of that ladder and suddenly I didn't simply want an empty bucket list as much as I want a to-love list for all this. *This* could be us. The wind could be in our hair like this, the sky wide with hope over us, the trials but stones on the way, and all the stones but steps higher up and deeper into God. We could be filled on the comfort food not of the world but the Word, enclosed in the broken-and-given of a vulnerable communion, and Love Himself would make us into love, pour us out, and make our hearts into a roof for others to absorb their beating storms. *Stego* . . . we could be a roof—a safe place.

Ours could be a vocation of translation, every enemy made an esteemed guest, every face encountered made the face of Christ—all this, all this living, made into the cruciformity of Christ. We could be buckets poured out and crushed into bread to feed the busted, and we could be dead to all ladders and never go higher, but only lower, to the lonely, the least, the longing, and the lost. That right there would be our love song.

He looks down the ladder at me, looks down from the edge of the roof. That four-day-old stubble of his carries a grin that speaks what you can only feel where the chambers of the heart meet. Yeah, there are those big-banner, social-media, camera-rolling moments with some imagined soundtrack building to a thundering crescendo, times when we think we'd all pour out our lives, throw ourselves out of a plane, in front of a train, show no restraint, and brave the howl of the hurricane to rescue love, to save our love.

But real love doesn't always look like that kind of heroism—that's more like Hollywood. Real love looks like a sacrificing Savior. That's the holy truth. The real romantics know that stretch marks are beauty marks and that different-shaped women fit into the different shapes of men's souls and that real romance is really *sacrifice.*

God is love. And because God is love, He gets to define love: "This is how we know what love is: Jesus Christ laid down his life for us."

Love is not always agreement with someone, but it is always sacrifice for someone.

Love only has logic, only has meaning, when it takes the form of the cross.

FOR REFLECTION

✧ How is your life's calling a vocation of translation, every enemy made an esteemed guest, every face encountered made the face of Christ, and all this, living, made into the cruciformity of Christ?

✧ How is your love looking cruciform? Because this is the abundant life.

Devotion 25

BORING LOVE

"Though it is the smallest of all seeds, yet when it grows, it is the largest of garden plants and becomes a tree, so that the birds come and perch in its branches."

MATTHEW 13:32

You do something great with your life when you do all the small things with His great love.

That black-inked cross, the one daily written on my wrist, it might cut into me like a tender surgery, break me and remake me, reform me cruciform. It all seemed embarrassingly small, how I ended up daily being the GIFT: complimenting an insecure kid, doing a messy chore, making a tired man's bed, taping a scrawled love note to a smudged and splattered mirror.

Why hadn't somebody showed up a long time ago in a three-piece suit to tell me those small acts of intentional love actually trigger the brain's receptor networks for oxytocin, the soothing hormone of maternal bonding? That little acts of large love actually release dopamine, that hormone associated with positive emotions and a natural high? Why hadn't anyone told me: bend low in small acts of love, and you get literally "high"?

Real love dares you to the really dangerous: *Die in the diminutive.* Be broken and given in the small, the moments so small no one may applaud at all. Pour out your life in laundry rooms and over toilets and tubs, and pour out life on the back streets, in the back of the room, back behind

107

the big lights. Pour out your life in small moments, because it's only these moments that add up to the monumental. The only way to live a truly remarkable life is not to get everyone to notice you, but to leave noticeable marks of His love everywhere you go.

Love is so large that it has to live in the holiness of very small moments of sacrifice. Love demands that you lie down and die in the small moments, the moments not scripted for screens but written into the inner hem of a heart that can change how someone breathes.

In the night stillness of our bedroom, his breath is warm and close. His fingers find mine. Our hands lace in the black, the promise we keep making, even in near-sleep: *I will let myself be bent into a roof for you, a shelter for you. I will be your roof. I will be your* stego—*your safe place. I will love you.*

It's this. I lie there thinking how it is all of this. The real romantics are the boring ones—they let another heart bore a hole deep into theirs. The broken way is the beautiful, boring way, the way two lives touch and go deeper into time with each other, one act of sacrificial love after another. The best love could be a broken, boring love—letting your heart be bore into by another heart, one small act of love at a time.

The way you touch the small of his back in the middle of the night when he can't find relief from the fever. The way he saves you a piece of strawberry pie. The way you hold your tongue quiet as a way of holding him. The way you slow and look right into the eyes of a child every time she speaks so they feel seen and known and safe. This is the love we all seek, and love is simple and small and complicated and a kind of boring and the largest of all and love is all there is.

It comes quiet. Real love is in the really small gestures—the way your hands, your feet, move to speak your heart.

FOR REFLECTION

✧ How does it change your perspective to be broken and given in the small—in the moments so small no one may applaud at all, but God sees?

✧ How are your hands and feet and life speaking the abundant love in your heart?

Devotion 26

PRACTICING PRESENCE

Be very glad—for these trials make you partners with Christ in his suffering, so that you will have the wonderful joy of seeing his glory when it is revealed to all the world.

1 PETER 4:13 NLT

Yeah, so Brother Lawrence has his sacred spuds.

And I've got this bag of rotting carrots pulling up a burial blanket of fleecing mold in the bottom of the fridge—and a bunch of girls making brownies and a sink overflowing with a motley crew of pots that have lost handles.

You can lose your precarious way by ten in the morning.

Yeah, they can crank the speakers right up on Sunday morning and play the worship music so loud your inner cochlea quakes for mercy and they can flash the three-point outline in pixels up there on the screen before the final prayer—but everybody ends up just going home to the kitchen to find something to eat.

Brother Lawrence and his potatoes are on to something: theology can be talked about on Sundays, recorded at conferences—but it's lived in kitchens or it dies at tables.

Doctrine in the kitchen is doctrine in real life. Don't belittle everyday pots and pans—they are the means to carry theology into the everyday of our lives.

The mother in the kitchen is the one who can actually give life to the words of the speaker on the platform. Platform words are dead words— until brave people live them out in the kitchen.

Two cousins pour and stir over the stove, loud and lovely; I count out a bunch of sweet spuds across the counter. There is light at the window.

What had that Brother Lawrence said in *The Practice of the Presence of God*? "The time of business . . . does not with me differ from the time of prayer, and in the noise and clatter of my kitchen, while several persons are at the same time calling for different things, I possess GOD in as great tranquillity as if I were upon my knees."[29] And, yeah, there are kids and there is loud and there is clatter but this is all that matters: when you have an overwhelmed world, you don't have to have an underwhelmed soul if Christ fills the thoughts.

Exhaling can feel like the beginning of a divine conversation. I exhale again. The girls measure out the butter, ask for a spatula. I rummage through a drawer, looking for the peeler for the sweet potatoes.

God's presence needs no practicing because God's presence has no end. God's presence needs no practicing because it's perfect and it's present everywhere. God's presence needs no practicing—we're the ones who need to practice waking to it. God's presence doesn't need practicing—His presence needs to be breathed.

Exhale.

You don't practice His presence. You practice being present to His presence in this present moment. Practicing the presence of God is the practice of self-discipline. In the midst of everything calling for my attention—the point is to never stop leaning into the One who is calling me.

"Can you find the measuring cup?" Shalom's holding the recipe card.

"Got it!" Her cousin laughs, holds vintage orange Tupperware up like a trophy.

I peel another strip off a sweet potato—and there it is, like a peeling of the heart: You miss Jesus when you don't look for Him in the right places . . .

Your soul misses Jesus when more time is spent on Facebook than face in the Book. Your soul misses Jesus when more time is spent on Instagram feeds than feeding on His Word. Your soul misses Jesus when more time is spent on Twitter chats than chatting with Jesus, whom you claim to follow. Balanced social media can be a soul meal; too much social media can be soul suicide.

Exhale.

The girls lean into each other over a 9 x 13 pan. I can feel that, how a soul can do that.

Every Christ follower is in the same business—to kill busy-ness and make it your business to talk endlessly with God. It's like the rhythm of breathing: *His presence. My gift. His presence. My gift.*

Exhale.

The girls lick out the bowl, and a big brother comes grinning for something to feed his hunger.

And there is light across the counters. Across the table, across the cutting boards, across the potatoes—there is this Light that can saturate anything.

FOR REFLECTION

✧ Are there ways your broken heart is missing Jesus? What might you do to change that?

✧ How are you living as the gift of His presence? Imagine living the next twenty-four hours as the gift of His presence. How might that look like more of the abundant life?

Devotion 27

GRIEVING BROKENNESS

*When he heard this, Jesus said, "This sickness will not end
in death. No, it is for God's glory so that God's Son may be
glorified through it."*

JOHN 11:4

Kneeling on the garden path, sun on my neck, in a brown and dead patch
of brittle kale, I keep tracing the outline of the bricks, finding a way. My
friend Elizabeth has died, her life poured right out. And I feel like I've failed
to love like I wanted to. And ever and always, I'd about give my eye teeth and
left arm for more time to get it more deeply right and less painfully wrong.

What happens if you just let the brokenness keep coming? Surrender.
Let the wave of it all break over you and wash you up at the foot of that
cross. What if I lived like I believed it: *never be afraid of broken things—
because Christ is redeeming everything.*

What if I began to feel? What if I let the dam of feelings break? It was
coming, and there was no stopping it. Grieving how plans change—is part
of the plan to change us. Elizabeth had broken something in me; she'd
broken me open to this reaching out to trace the face of suffering, to feel
along its features—and I hadn't wanted to recoil, but at times, it felt too
much, too vulnerable, to live broken into life like that. But what if I didn't
recoil from this? What if I didn't pull back from the pain?

I wanted to be more—more patient, to never lose it, to always have it together, to keep calm and sane. I've wanted more flashes of wisdom in the heat of the moment when I had no bloody idea what was the best thing to do. I've wanted fewer nights crawling into bed feeling like a failure who always gets it wrong when everyone else seems to get it right. I've wanted to take the gold medal in living well and loving large and being enough to be wanted. Instead, I've been the person who escapes behind bathroom doors, the person who turns on the water so no one can hear the howl, the person who fights what is and struggles to surrender, who completely ups and forgets how to break into givenness.

And there's the razor edge of it: I am not someone who once walked nice and neat on this narrow way, and then suddenly didn't. I'm not someone who just tripped and stumbled a bit, but then pulled herself back up on the narrow path. I'm the person who's always been shattered on the inside, knowing brokenness deep in the marrow and ache of me, the one who has wasted days, years, despairing and replaying the past, who's let lies live loud in my head, held grudges, and grown bitter, who's cut myself down, literally, and known depression, suicidal and self-sabotaging self-destruction, and been convinced she would so keenly feel like a broken failure in the end that she'd wish she had never been born.

Feelings of failure can be like this bad rash—scratch one failure and all you can see is an outbreak spreading all over you. Can I choke it out, how this trying to love, how this surrendering to being cruciform—which is what love is—can feel like being lashed to an altar and your bare back stinging a bit raw? How there are times you'd like to cut and break free and run, only to realize you'd be running into meaninglessness—which would only hurt and break you more. What if you just want desperately, in spite of everything, for someone to remember how hard you've really tried?

There are days when the sharp edge of self-condemnation cuts you so deep that you can be reaching, grasping, but can't seem to remember to believe that He believes in you. *God, make us the re-membering people.*

Maybe the only way to begin breaking free is to lay open your willing hands and bear witness to the ugly mess of your scars. To trace them slowly and re-member what He says about you, even if you forget. This is about bravely letting our darkness be a canvas for God's light. *This happened that the glory of God might be shown through even you.*[30]

What if the re-membering of your brokenness comes in remembering that your trying isn't what matters the most, because His scars have written your name and your worth over all of yours?

There's this breaking, this spilling, for all that hasn't been. All that I haven't been. The lament and the grieving and the repentance all mingle. Feelings are meant to be fully felt and then fully surrendered to God. The word *emotion* comes from the Latin for "movement"—and all feelings are meant to move you toward God.

What if I fully surrendered to becoming cruciform so I could feel along my scars, along my own scarred face, and know my own name is Beloved? I don't know if there's any other way to break into abundant living unless I come to *know* this.

All this failing rises from the ground of the kitchen garden toward heaven, bits of dead kale leaves breaking and falling in hardly a whisper of wind. The garden path bricks feel like a kind of beckoning forward under my tracing fingertips, my bent knees.

I don't turn away—grief can feel like an aching love song.

FOR REFLECTION

- ✧ How does it change your life to know that your trying is not what matters the most, but that Christ's scars have written your name and your worth over all of your scars?
- ✧ How are you fully surrendered to becoming cruciform, having a life that is cross-shaped so you can feel along your scars and know your own name is Beloved?

COMPASSIONATE ABUNDANCE

Be kind to one another, tenderhearted, forgiving one another,
as God in Christ forgave you.

EPHESIANS 4:32 ESV

If you lean in close, you can hear it. Folks despairing from rejection right now. Some conflicted and confused. And some deeply grieving. There is deep divide and painful brokenness all around us. There is very real fear and pain, and the call is always not to dismiss each other, only take time to listen to each other.

When we feel forgotten and dismissed, we become trapped in pain. And how many people feel painfully forgotten and dismissed? Many people hold their positions the way they do because of genuine fear for their future. And then different people end up genuinely feeling their own kind of fear for their futures.

Strange how that is. We are all the same kind of different. Family may disagree, but they still agree that they are a family.

Maybe the way forward in the midst of division and the brokenness is always to give forward. Maybe right now, instead of giving someone a piece of your mind, it's far better to give them pieces of your heart. Maybe right now, we go forward by *giving it forward today*. And maybe it never mattered more than it does today: *be the GIFT* and give someone the benefit of the doubt.

Involved in a group conversation? Go out of your way to make sure each person feels included. Grab a group of friends and serenade strangers on the street. Reach out across dividing lines and say hi to a friend who might be a little different than you. Let them know you love them for who they are, not how they hold certain positions.

Take a photo of anything you see that reminds you of someone and send it their way. It's a healing way to say, "Thinking of you!" Stand on a street corner for ten minutes and give compliments to everyone you see. Reach out to someone today who is feeling hurt, who is grieving. Listen well. Find one person today who is "other," who thinks differently, lives differently, sees things differently. And just do that: listen to each other, listen to the "other."

Maybe if each of us, everywhere, could find just one person who is the "other" today and really listen until the "other" feels understood—this is what it means when Jesus said, "Love one another"—to love *the other*.

Absurd comes from the Latin word *surdus*, which means "deaf." Things will only become more absurd if we don't listen but instead grow deaf to each other. Whenever we deafen, demonize, and dehumanize anybody, we can legitimize anything. It's the Latin word that means "listening," *audire*, that gives us the word *obedient*. An abundant life is a listening life.

Listening fully to each other is how to be fully obedient to God. The only way to a sincerely God-obedient life is to live a sincerely listening life. In the midst of the brokenness, now is the time, for such a time, to listen to each other, so that we can be known for how well we love each other. This might be a step toward the healing we all agree is needed desperately and desperately wanted.

We may not understand each other, but we can stand with each other. Instead of dismissing each other out of hand, now is the time to reach out a hand and deeply listen to each other. If we all made it a practice to genuinely listen every day to one person with whom we disagree, we'd get to genuinely practice our faith.

Maybe God's purposes come not so much through power but through the compassion of God's people. Compassion is more powerful than power. Ask Jesus, who chose to die on a cross. Compassion, co-passion, literally means co-suffering. And co-suffering with the suffering is how Jesus chose to transform suffering. If we could be compassionate with each other—co-suffer with each other—we could be part of the healing of each other.

If we are passionate about the church having any transformational power in the world, then the call of the church is to be compassionate—to live cruciform. Formed like a cross, we take the form of reaching hands, open ears, listening hearts.

Because our God is with us, we will be with each other. Because our God is on the throne, we will not spout off with each other but will be on our knees for each other. Because our compassionate God is all-powerful, we will be compassionate with each other, because this is the way of the most powerful. Because our God is close to the brokenhearted, we will be near to the hearts of all the broken of all of us.

If you lean in close, in the warming autumn days you can hear it, like the heartbeat of hope: people coming together to give grace to each other, to be the gift to each other, the brokenness of things being re-membered in the remembering that there's no way to deny anyone a lavish glass of grace from which we ourselves have drunk lavishly.

FOR REFLECTION

- ✧ How is Jesus calling you, especially in the midst of your brokenness, to love the other, listen to the other, live given to the other?
- ✧ What would it look like in your life if you chose the way of being abundantly compassionate with each other—co-suffering with each other—so you could be part of the abundant healing of each other?

Devotion 29

ZACCHAEUS BROKENNESS

When Jesus reached the spot, he looked up and said to him, "Zacchaeus, come down immediately. I must stay at your house today." So he came down at once and welcomed him gladly.

LUKE 19:5–6

When she stopped returning my calls, my texts, I'm not going to lie, it kinda felt like I'd lost a compass, like I'd lost my way home to a safe place. I couldn't get over the anxiety of feeling lost—abandoned. Unwanted. Left.

Turns out that when you're ghosted, you're the one who wants to up and disappear. I didn't eat for days. Anxiety can make for a strict diet. Maybe part of me wondered if I stopped eating, didn't open my mouth, I could fade away, make myself and the pain of being me invisible.

Sometimes when you look in the mirror, it's self-hatred staring back at you. I'd look in the mirror long—turn away when everything started to blur. How had I failed so miserably again, botched it completely again, hurt someone deeply again? Sometimes when your relationships all feel broken, the person you want to break up with most is yourself. Sometimes the hardest person for whom to hold out any hope for change—is yourself.

It can feel like there's nowhere to go to escape the sting of rejection. I dreamed about flying to Iceland. Instead I drove into town and bought groceries at Food Basics.

You know the people who'd avoid you in the grocery store. Who'd look the other way if they saw you in the parking lot, people who'd mutter and not turn the other cheek but turn away, act like they don't know you.

I kept having painful Zacchaeus moments. Zacchaeus moments are those moments of rejection. When we feel as disliked and shunned as a tax collector. When we feel like no one would come to our house, ask us for lunch, or look for us in the crowd.

Tax collectors collected no one's warmth, friendship, or esteem. And yet six times the socially rejected tax collectors are mentioned in the book of Luke—and *every single time, positively*. It's a pattern to weave the ends of your frayed heart to: Jesus is drawn to the rejected and the rejected are drawn to Jesus.

And it's the people who draw themselves up as the respectable who find Jesus repelling. Why?

Because when you feel basically respectable, you want *religion*. And when you know you feel the brokenness of rejection, you want the *gospel*. In religion, it's the "respectable" who search for a God to impress. But in the gospel, it's God who searches for the brokenhearted rejected to *save*.

The only "respectable" who become Christians—are those who realize they aren't. It's not that *even* the rejected are accepted by Jesus—but it's that *only* the rejected are accepted by Jesus, only those who confess that using their self-sufficiency and supposed morality as seeming saviors is as sinful as any other sin. Only when you realize you *aren't* respectable, that you are entirely no better than the rejected—only then are you entirely accepted.

Jesus states it with relieving audacity straight into the ache of our hearts when he turns to Zacchaeus in his moment: "Today salvation has come to this house."[31] Not that salvation *will* come, but salvation *has* come—because Jesus is here. You don't have to perform, or be perfect, or pretend. You have to know a *Person*—One who pursues you. Jesus doesn't give Zacchaeus a checklist before He'll show up. Christ just shows up, right where we are, right in the midst of our brokenness. Salvation isn't about keeping rules. It's about keeping at rest in the work of Christ, keeping company with the grace of Christ, keeping your joy through the strength of Christ. Salvation is a way of seeing—seeing who your Savior always is.

Like Zacchaeus, there's a way to position your heart to see Christ in all things. Zacchaeus had to climb the limbs of a tree; we get to climb over everything else in our lives to turn the pages of Scriptures and sit with Him who wants to be with us. *Abundant acceptance is possible.*

Zacchaeus had to make himself look less than respectable to see Jesus—and we get to be seen as less than respectable to actually be more like Jesus. *Abundant joy is possible.*

If we've positioned our lives to see Jesus, we get to go to the rejected, eat with the less than respected, make time for the rundown and the reviled and the rebuffed. *Abundant fulfillment is possible.*

Zacchaeus had turned around to go Christ's way and thus turned around his attitude toward money; we get to be born again and have Christ cut our umbilical security cord to money and status and hollow meaninglessness. *Abundant freedom is possible.*

These are the words of Christ to the brokenhearted, all of us stuck in a string of Zacchaeus moments: "I must stay at your house today."

He must. The Brokenhearted Healer must stay with the broken—His home is with you.

So this is *our* Zacchaeus moment, us, the broken—abundantly accepted. Communion with Christ, *koinonia* with the King, who comes to stay with the busted and rejected, and we "received Him joyfully."[32]

Because Jesus tenderly claims the rejected, bandages the bruised, carries the exiled, names the unwanted His, and holds the hemorrhaging close.

Those shoved to the outside know the gentleness of His embrace.

Those stabbed in the back find their hearts cupped.

Those avoided and abandoned feel an intimate communion with the Wounded Healer. The fellowship of the broken have fellowship with the Brokenhearted Healer—and by His wounds we are healed.

The courage to embrace suffering is a way to embrace Him—the One who never stops suffering with us, Immanuel, the With-God, who stretches out His arms on a cross, to show us His scars too, to expose His heart too, to be vulnerable too, to hold us and literally save us too.

The With-God holds whatever our unspoken broken is and cups our faces and whispers, "Me too." The With-God is the Me-Too God.

And when He must come stay at my house today, when He must come stay with me—no matter how many painful Zacchaeus moments I have known—I am abundantly found.

I am always already home.

FOR REFLECTION

⬦ What painful, brokenhearted Zacchaeus moments would you like to invite Jesus into today—moments of feeling rejected, belittled, dismissed? Jesus wants to make His home with you in those places.

⬦ How are you positioning your life, the abundant life, like Zacchaeus so that you see Christ in all things, even if it costs you something?

Devotion 30

CRISIS GIVENNESS

For the LORD *your God is a compassionate God; He will not fail you nor destroy you nor forget the covenant with your fathers which He swore to them.*

DEUTERONOMY 4:31 NASB

H e'd woken up looking ashen when our 2016 was hardly more than twenty-four hours old. Grey, translucent skin. Sunken eyes, like bruised, blue half-moons, his shirt hanging angular off bony shoulders.

Yet the kid never left the table without asking for second and third heaping helpings. A robust farm boy of thirteen eating like he was famished, and yet fading away.

I don't know when I knew. But I knew before the doctor on call told us.

Snow had started to fall, large flakes, lazy and soft and soundless.

The Farmer squeezes my hand. "All God's plans are always good, and all His ways are always for us." I know it. The words aren't some cheap cliché, but are our dying creed, and I swallow hard round that stone lodged up in my throat. "It didn't really hit me," he says, "until the doctor came in and sat down on the end of his bed and said it so quiet: 'You have Type 1 diabetes. You'll need four to six insulin injections a day for the rest of your life.'"

This isn't the flu and we beat this virus. There's no cure. No pills, no diet, no exercise will ever make it go away.

I squeeze his weathered hand back. You can feel like you've been flattened by a bus. You can feel like everyone else is mapping out their future and you're standing there with the map, looking for the red arrow that points to where in the world you even are now. You can make your plans, but it's God's plans that happen. You can blink, and the landscape of your whole life can change, and how do you not look a little bit lost? "I feel like we just joined a club," I say. This club of the hurting-in-hidden-ways, and those beating back the grave.

We can't rank or minimize suffering, and we must simply embrace suffering and all those suffering. And it's okay to not be okay, to not feel strong, to carry an unspoken broken. It's okay to be real and grieve losses and hold each other tight. He and I hold on to each other in the dim light of the hospital rooms, alarms going off down the hall.

Later, Malakai pushes himself up in the hospital bed to tell us something I will never forget: "Looks like God knew my story was going to be a bit different—and that's sorta cool."

He smiles quietly, nods like he's telling places in me of forgotten things.

"And this hard thing's going to make me rely on Him more—and that's even more cool."

I nod. Yeah, son—cool.

Never fear the moments you imagine will freeze you: unexpected blasts of cold can be what draws you nearer to the flame of His love.

Darn the cold. Thank God for the fire. Welcome to the club of those braving the cold blasts in a thousand daily ways.

"He's real." The kid's nodding his head. "I've never felt God so real."

I wanna tell the kid that's what happens when you get pushed out of the shallow end. When you find yourself in the real deep end, that's when you know He's real. *Adios*, shallow end. Now you live where you can't touch bottom—and you must swallow God.

"I can see that, Mom." He's smiling. "The hardest things can be the greatest gift. I can see that."

The kid's seeing things. Things I forget, things that can feel like a mirage at times for me. He's feeling solid in things that I've let slip through my rope-burned fingers; he's holding on to it now, like a lifeline in his brave hand.

Malakai grins over at me, needle still in hand: "I am glad. I am glad God gave me joy."

I want to write it down on my hand to remember: Brave joy is the magnet for everything you need. The boy knows things I need to relearn.

I sit on the edge of his bed, trying to read the kid's eyes, my heart trying to Braille-read what his heart's really saying by the way his eyes make my heart feel.

The kid's got no idea that the new normal means heading down to the pediatric hospital, where he'll sit with his needles in the waiting room with rows of brave kids with bald, gleaming heads sitting on their mamas' laps, and you'll look into those mamas' eyes and be loving this club of the broken with all your heart.

Every one of us, in one hurting way or another, is in this club. The grace that's in this moment is your manna. Wish for the past and you drink poison. Worry about the future and you eat fire. Stay in this moment and you eat the manna needed for now.

When I stand out in the hallway reading about how after a year or so doctors may allow an insulin pump and thinking about stirring pots of chili with one hand and giving injections with the other, refusing to be sucked into the worry of the future, I read: "Type 1 diabetes . . . may reduce the normal lifespan by ten to fifteen years."

And I think of ten full spins around the sun, ten more puffs over birthday candles, ten more first days of spring and how March sun feels on your face. I want him to wake every morning. I want him to have those full ten.

I want all the hurting and brave in the club that is all of us to beat the odds, beat back the dark, and find their hope against despair. I want us to pummel worry with worship, all of us to make every move with courage while everybody else moves on. I want this club to inhale fresh air and have another glass of orange juice right now and taste the phenomenon of *being*, and feel wind through the hair and believe that what you *love* will come to you in your hour of need, and this one glorious day is a miracle—why do we get two?

It falls like fresh snow in the middle of the night, like the steady beat of the heart, like the rhythm of our being: *This life of ours is not our own—He owns our life. This life of ours is not our own—His life is our own. This life of ours is not our own—we are His own.*

And I turn from the night window and the falling snow to our boy sleeping in a hospital bed the second day of the new year: there's the club of the broken, who ask, "So what if we suffer? Here is not our home." Suffering is a gift He entrusts, and He can be trusted to make this suffering into a gift. Stay in this moment and eat the manna needed for now.

His eyelashes tremble a bit in his sleep. Even in dreams, all of life is holy ground. Come morning, the snow gives way to the light, like the abundant hope of a lifting shroud.

──────── FOR REFLECTION ────────

- ✧ Where feels broken in your life right now? What would it mean to consider suffering as a gift and to believe that God can be trusted to make this suffering into a gift?
- ✧ How are you living like brave joy is the magnet for the abundance of everything you need?

126

Part Four

How Can the Brokenhearted Find Real Communion?

Devotion 31

THE GIVERS

"Give, and it will be given to you. A good measure, pressed down, shaken together and running over, will be poured into your lap. For with the measure you use, it will be measured to you."

LUKE 6:38

When Aimee got up to the drive-through window, she flicked her dark hair back, leaned out of her minivan, and said to the girl behind the glass, "And can I go ahead and pay for the car behind me?"

Then she turned to me with this knowing, bright glint in her eye. "You know, it goes this way every time. When you give it forward, you get paid back the most."

When David, just the other day, found Russell curled up on the floor, sobbing behind a ticket counter at Reno-Tahoe International Airport, David kneeled down, reached straight through Russell's autism, gently touched his shoulder, and assured him he'd help reroute him to make his destination.

And when he'd found a new flight, David returned to hold and rock Russell, even bringing the pilot to assure him they could arrange seating for Russell's comfort and the crew would give safe passage—he need not be afraid.

Every one of us is a member of humanity; we support all of our members and stop the dismembering of society. Just show up and show the grace

129

you're made of. Stand apart from an overheated world through showing understanding. Show you give a rip by giving a bit of your heart.

Kristina, a single mom, flat broke, sleeping on the floor of her kids' room and filling her fridge with food stamps groceries, said, "When you don't know if you're good for the rent, it's easy to get thinking that life isn't good."

When you're obsessed with your own despair, it's easy to get depressed with your own life. Sometimes the only way to get out of your skin is to get into someone else's story. Sometimes helping other people helps our own wounds. Sometimes the way out of your misery is to help someone else out of theirs. It's strange how that works: volunteering can be a way to joy finding you voluntarily.

The secrets of the world work in upside-down, unlikely ways because the Maker of this world is unlike anything we've ever known.

The Maker has this wildly warped and holy sense of humor. Every volunteer place rejected Kristina because no place wanted her kids coming with her. When no one wants you, it can be hard to want to be you.

But Kristina talked to herself—because we always need to talk to ourselves more than we *listen* to ourselves, because our soul needs a truth coach or it will be a lie factory: "Even when I feel like a complete loser, is there something tiny I am still good at?"

And she realized, *I know how to cook a great meal—on very little money.* So Kristina cooked up an idea. She emailed friends: "Every Wednesday night I'm feeding people." Widows. The elderly. Singles. The lonely.

Everyone was important enough. She wouldn't focus on what she *couldn't give* but on *what she could give* and *who* she could give to.

Her food stamps bought anything on sale, and with no recipes in hand, just the vision to make the greatest feast with the least amount of money, Kristina did it.

Sometimes the least in hand can make the greatest happiness in the heart. Because having much in hand doesn't make as much difference as having much in heart.

When it looks like you have nothing to give naturally, look to God to give the supernatural.

When the lies came—*Why would anyone show up at your place? Why would your friends bring anyone to you?*—she ignored them. When you're depressed, you can feel like you have nothing to bring to the table but a mess.

But Wednesday at 6 p.m., people came to her table.

"Complete strangers, walking into my apartment and letting me feed them. By the end of the night, I had fed a ton of strangers with my tiny little budget, and my tiny little kids."

When you give when you don't have a lot, God gives you a lot more of Himself. When you give because you've claimed a stake in your Father's abundant world, *you get an abundant world of joy.* When your giving and living debunks the myth of scarcity and embraces the mystery of abundance, *you get the joy of intimacy—with God.*

After the last person left, she closed the door and started sobbing. But for the first time in a long time, it wasn't tears of desperation. "I was crying like a broken little girl who just experienced her first glimmer of hope and healing," she said.

It's the broken who become healers. It's the givers and gifters who get to recover from the hard knocks and hard roads; it's the givers and gifters who get to take back their joy; it's the gifters and givers who get to overcome whatever overwhelms, because Love gives and that's how love wins, and our God is the Giver who loved the world so much that He gave.

Be an Aimee, a David, a Kristina, a broken healer, a giver, a gifter.

Be the bread so broken and given that a hungry world yearns for more of the taste of such glory.

FOR REFLECTION

✧ Where have you felt too broken for your gifts to be wanted? And where do you feel like you have nothing naturally to give, but God is asking you to let Him give the supernatural?

✧ Where have you been living the myth of scarcity and God is asking you to be a giver and a gifter and live the mystery of abundance?

Devotion 32

LIVING GIVEN

*"In the same way, let your light shine before others, that they
may see your good deeds and glorify your Father in heaven."*

MATTHEW 5:16

Jamie-Lynn stood at the checkout aisle of Trader Joe's with a baby
slung on her hip and couldn't find even a dime in her purse. She needed
$200 for the bill and her cart of groceries. Debit card at home, credit card
declined, and the baby had to be howling in her ear.

Matthew Jackson stepped out of line. "Let me cover it."

You know—let your shortcomings be covered with long kindnesses.
Jamie-Lynn refused. Matthew insisted. *Please.*

She looked up and could see it in Matthew Jackson's eyes: he meant
it. The kid meant it.

"Look, you don't have to pay me back." Matthew Jackson pulled out
his wallet. "Just give it forward."

Truth is: we can't pay it back—we can only give it forward. And this
is the same thing. There are times we get to restore each other to strength.

Yes, Jamie-Lynn said, yes, she would give it forward, and she scribbled
down his name and where he worked so she could thank him again.
Somehow.

A week later, Jamie-Lynn rang up Matthew's boss. Could she stop by
to thank Matthew—offer some gift of thanks?

"Matthew's dead," he said. "Car accident last week—not far from that Trader Joe's."

I heard it once said: "You cannot do a kindness too soon, for you never know how soon it will be too late."

Less than twenty-four hours after Matthew had paid her bill, his car wrapped around a tree and his heart slammed to a stop. But he didn't die when he struck that tree because this is how the universe works: give love and you always stay alive, even after you're gone. Kindness multiplies each time it's shared, grows until it becomes a blazing act of heroic courage, much later and far away.

Jamie-Lynn was heartbroken, but nothing could stop her from keeping her promise to him to give his grace forward. She told people about Matthew's gift of kindness and she asked them to give it forward—and they did! Glorious people, from small town, back road, and every side of this spinning world, giving it forward. Driving cancer patients to the hospital and donating blood and reading to kids down at the library and having a coffee ready for the mail carrier and handing out flowers at the gas station and buying the milk for the woman in the checkout line. People gave forward the act of kindness Matthew Jackson began.

Small things can change everything, even when we feel like we have nothing to give. Every one of us can start changing headlines when we start reaching out our hands.

They gave in Scotland, in Wisconsin, in Australia. "Overwhelming," Jamie-Lynn said. "It was overwhelming."

When Matt was a kid, his mom said, they stopped once under a sweltering hot Phoenix sun to get a cold bottle of water. But one stoplight later, Matthew had flung himself out of the car straight toward a panhandler, thrusting his still-sealed bottle into the stunned stranger's hand.

"I knew my boy was like this," she said.

I'd sat with that. Whose example are we taking up? Be so intimate with Christ, your life could be imitated.

Don't doubt that there are angels. Don't doubt He could make you like one. Love only grows in the world when we all share love. Love only grows by giving, by being broken and given like bread. We all only get more of the lives we want by giving away bits of the lives and love we have.

The world may get divisive, but what changes the world is when we divide and multiply amazing grace. The grace of holding open a door, of nodding a kind smile, a willing patience that lets someone go ahead, of giving it forward today in the smallest ways—even when you feel you have nothing to give.

Giving isn't about what you have in your hands; it's what you have in your heart. Never doubt it: an act of kindness, giving it forward, can be more powerful than a sword in starting needed revolutions.

People may be angry—give them love anyway. People may not like your way—give them kindness anyway. People may disagree with you—give them space at the table anyway.

The world could be full of Matthew's people, the way ahead blazing like every act, and every person can be filled with His abundant Light.

For Reflection

✧ Because giving isn't about what you have in your hands—it's what you have in your heart—what do you have in your broken heart today that you could choose to give forward?

✧ If we all only get more of the abundant life we want by giving away bits of the lives and love we have, how would that change your day? Your priorities? Your life?

Devotion 33

"If Only" Brokenness

Who shall separate us from the love of Christ? Shall trouble
or hardship or persecution or famine or nakedness or danger
or sword? . . . No, in all these things we are more than
conquerors through him who loved us.

ROMANS 8:35, 37

I'd do anything to get back there and do it all over again. If only . . ."
She turns away, squeezing my hand tight. Her fingers smudge the inked
cross on my wrist.

Oh, Mama. That may be the saddest string of words that's ever been
strung together: *"If only . . ."*

I can taste the words in my mouth. Who doesn't know *"if only . . ."*?

If only there was time for me to go back for do-overs of my own, say
different things to the kids, only speaking words that make souls stronger,
somehow live better, love realer. If only grief hadn't driven my mother a
kind of hurting crazy into psych wards all through my childhood. If only
my sister's skull hadn't been crushed like tender fruit by a delivery truck
in front of all our helpless eyes. If only I hadn't kept a stuffed closet full
of a thousand ugly sins. *If only . . .*

But there's no way back. Maybe life always tastes a bit like regret.
Whatever you do or don't do, there is no way to never taste it. And though
you may have to taste regret, you don't have to believe in it—you don't

have to live in it, like rowing a boat that only goes backward, trying to find something that's been washed out to sea. It's God's sea. And that means all is grace.

Mama's cheeks are wet. I'm standing there like a fool looking into my own sadness over what can't now be—*because I haven't been all I could have been.* She's my mama, and I'm her daughter. And now I'm a mama, and we both have never stopped laboring, wondering if we will ever fully know deliverance into abundance.

Mama and I, we're sitting here at her kitchen table, kids waiting out in the van for me, and I can see the suffering right there in Mama's eyes, what she's doing to herself. I know because I'd just been the busted and broken doing it myself. How do you beg people to love you when you least deserve it, because that's when you need it the most—and what if that's exactly what God does?

How do you survive if you don't turn on the enemy of your soul and call him by what his ugly name really means: *prosecutor*? The very name *Satan* literally means "prosecutor." And his work isn't ultimately to tempt you, but to *try* you.

"Mama?" Her cheek feels like wrinkled silk. "Please hear me. All that was intended to harm, God intended all of it for good. All that's been, no matter what was intended to harm you, God's arms have you."

Not one of us is ever too broken. "Give our Lord the benefit of believing that His hand is leading you, and accept the anxiety of feeling yourself in suspense and incomplete," assures Pierre Teilhard de Chardin.[33]

Without even thinking, my fingers find my wrist where I once cut, and the tips of me trace that cross, and even Joseph's suffering was the door into discovering more of God.[34] Suffering that does not break us away from more of this world and break us into more of God is wasted suffering.

Become that cross. Cruciform.

Later, after she's found comfort and I've found the grace of her smile, I try to memorize the sound of the girls' voices in the backseat on the way home, the string of starlings on the telephone lines. I try to be present to grace. The photos seemed to make me feel it: the past is a memory sealed right into you, tomorrow is a mystery unknown to you, and today is God's momentary gift to you—which is why it's called the present.

Continuously make Christ present. I've got a cross in this inky scrawl, right there on my wrist.

Make Christ present. Become cruciform.

FOR REFLECTION

✧ How could you take "if only" regrets and brokenness and let them break you away from more of this world and break you into more of God—so that your brokenness and suffering isn't wasted suffering?

✧ What if you drew a cross on your wrist today, every day this week, as a visual to make Christ present, to become cruciform—would you be willing to take the dare for more of the abundant life?

Devotion 34

ENTERING ABUNDANCE

But our citizenship is in heaven. And we eagerly await a
Savior from there, the Lord Jesus Christ.

PHILIPPIANS 3:20

S omeone has to be that mother.

That mother who drives a full three hours to the border with a packed minivan and anxious kids and creeps through a twenty-minute traffic backup under the hot, beating sun—only to riffle through her wallet and look up feebly to tell the customs officer she doesn't have birth certificates for two of her children.

So that would be me.

"Do you have any ID at all—for either one of them?"

The customs officer asks it gently. Like he doesn't want to push the flustered and flailing over any imagined or very real edge.

He glances back at the long snake of vehicles behind me, waiting. In the sun. That's not moving either.

"Um . . . no." I shuffle through my wallet again. "No, sir—I don't." Does the earth open up and swallow the Abiram of mothers?[35]

"I'm so sorry, sir. If I can just turn around?" I close my wallet and I can feel it up the neck, the face—the mother shame burning like a red-hot brand. How in the world? What kind of mother . . . ?

I'm already cranking at the steering wheel, trying to get this mess turned around, thinking that when you can't swallow down any grace, you turn yourself back from the land of the free.

"Just a moment, ma'am. Open up the door here." He waves my passport in the direction of the van's side door. I fumble behind me, try to unlatch it, still hoping the earth might open up instead. The officer pops his head in. "Birthdates, kids."

Birthdates?

Joshua states his month, day, year. Our daughter, Hope, leans forward and I'm the realist who doesn't hold out much hope at all.

The officer taps it into his computer, glances over at me. "And are they Canadian citizens?"

"Yes?"

And I really try to say it like I'm not always a tentative Canadian, like it's not a question, like I think he's just gleefully extending the torture of my ineptness and lack of papers—because isn't this the United States of America, and when exactly did they start letting in farm hicks without a passport, without a birth certificate?

He looks up from the screen.

"Welcome to the United States, ma'am. Have a nice day."

And he hands me my passport.

"Welcome?" *Um . . . really?* "But if you let us into the States"—I stammer it out—"will Canada let us back in next week?"

"Well, if they are really Canadian citizens"—the officer nods, smiling—"they can't be denied entry."

I sit there shaking my head, stunned, and the officer keeps nodding his head *yes*. And I'm thinking, is entry in always firstly a matter of where you are born—and being born again?

Twelve miles down the road and the kids and I are still laughing stunned wonder right out loud, *"Thank You, Lord; thank You, Lord; thank You, Lord!"*

There's a grace that lets the impossible and failing in, and how can we ever get over this?

We pass a church and its steeple pointing the way home. We turn a corner where a yellow house bursts like a full summer sun. We drive by horses in a field with tails blowing free, with the sky big and round and circling, like the lid being lifted right off, and I feel this:

In Christ, you're a native of heaven right now. You aren't a citizen of here trying to work into heaven. You're a citizen of *heaven* trying to work through *here*.

The sky keeps unfolding all down the road. When your ethnicity is heaven, then all adversity offers the gift of intimacy, driving you into the home of His heart.

I'm a mess and I keep driving, smiling, and I know my citizenship and where this road leads. *Who in the world gets over this?*

There are hills and there are detours and there is this getting lost and it feels so late and it can creep in every day like the dusk, this feeling like a failure, and there is Scripture in the stereo, hope in His Word, and I try to remember to breathe, lost and right turned around.

Because this is always true: all my brokenness is a whisper that I don't belong, and every time I don't feel like I belong, the Scarred and Rejected God whispers, "Come here, My beloved."

And the longer I live, the more I feel like an exile. This is a gift. The exiled make His extravagant, abundant love their home.

We were made for heaven and Him, and our heart beats hard for it.

Somewhere in upstate New York, the skies thunder. A vehicle pulls out in front of us. I read the license plate: "LOOK2HIM."

And the skies and the heavens are above and close and coming down all around and we're all out here in the rain and His reign and we're born again in Him and we are His and we are found.

In Christ—no matter the road, the storm, the story—we always know the outcome.

Our Savior: surrounds.

Our future: secure.

Our joy: certain.

And when a week brings us back to the border again—and we cross the bridge without two birth certificates—I'm praying, praying God's grace and Canadian customs will let us in.

When heaven is really your motherland, then prayer is really your mother tongue, and you can't help but yearn to speak in the language of your Father now.

As I pull into the line for customs, praying they'll let us home, Joshua yells it from behind me—"Rainbow!"

Really? It's like a welcome home!

"No—no, it's not a rainbow," says Joshua, and I don't have to see him behind my driver's seat to know how his voice, his eyes are searching, reading everything above.

"It's a *double* rainbow."

And I glance over my shoulder—and it's right there in living color like a signed vow straight across the sky.

Right there as I pull up to Canadian customs, and I tell a doubtful officer my ridiculous grace story, show her my passport, and the Canadian customs officer shakes her head. "I can't believe they let you in."

There's this double rainbow arching over us right there.

All I have is what I believe and the living of it, and His promises are abundantly enough.

There isn't a loss on earth that can ever rob us of the *abundant* riches our Lord has saved us for in Him.

And there's no getting over this miracle of entering into the country of our citizenship, of the failing belonging in Him and His Grace—all the heavens low and open and waiting and all the sky this flag.

This flag flying in the unwavering hues of the promise of home.

For Reflection

- ✧ Write down all the ways you feel broken in this season, the ways you feel you don't belong, and then sit in silence until you know in your bones how the Scarred and Rejected God whispers, "Come here, My beloved."

- ✧ How would you experience more of a meaningful, abundant life if you lived like you really believed that, in Christ, you're a native of heaven right now? You aren't a citizen of here trying to work into heaven; you're a citizen of *heaven* trying to work through *here*.

ABUNDANCE FROM ASHES

For you know the grace of our Lord Jesus Christ, that though he was rich, yet for your sake he became poor, so that you through his poverty might become rich.

2 CORINTHIANS 8:9

When I woke up yesterday morning, three fire stations and dozens of firefighters were out on the highway, wielding water hoses at flames licking out the windows of a little country church around the corner here.

Smoke threaded from the steeple straight up the sky like an ashen seam between heaven and earth. And I wondered, *Did God's Word light the place on fire? Were there ashes around the pulpit? Could the passion that lights fire in our bones leave a trail of ashes through our lives?*

Then a teenager told me the hardest things last night. And a woman I've prayed with for years, she told me her husband looked her in the eyes yesterday and said, "I don't love you anymore," and she curled up in a fetal ball on the bathroom floor and sobbed and wondered how abandonment can feel like being torn from the warmth of a womb and you're left gasping to breathe, how it can feel like a cold wind on your bare back and there's no one who can shield you from the relentless chill.

I had no words, could only feel this ember burning up my throat.

Our baby cry-howled through the night last night. I rocked her through the shadowed hours and thought of mothers around the world who rock their sick and feverish babies, and all across your center you can feel the slow scorching of this old broken world. Suffering is at the burning core of the world—because love is at the core of the world.

I stood once on the side of a mountain, beside a burn-scorched sequoia tree. Stood there running my hands along the ruddy bark of that burn-scarred tree. Flames had once licked the blackened earth, the bark of trees crackling, all this smoke rising up through the blazing forest like an ascension. In the western Sierra Nevadas, this one tree stood in the heat of the burn, in the searing blaze of the rising flame. And when the smoke cleared, seven thousand feet up that mountain, that one wonder of a tree still stands in an island of life, in a charred desolation.

The bark of that tree under my hand, it had the thickest skin, bark that grows up to twenty-four inches thick—the thickest bark of any tree on earth—and every single fire it endures burns away its competition for sunlight, and it's the fire that makes a fertilizer for the sequoia tree's growth. This fertilizer, otherwise known as ashes.

Standing there with my hand on a sequoia, the largest living organism on earth, hand on a tree, its inner rings scarred with hundreds of fires, it grows like a reverberation in me: *Do. Not. Ever. Be. Afraid. Of. Ashes.* And at the foot of the cross, you can hear the same message. What seems like ashes in your life can be the actual fertilizer that grows your life. Souls grow most in soil made rich by ashes. Fire makes a fertilizer for growth, and ashes can be the best soil for the best soul growth.

But how? How do you have no fear of the flame? That flame of the unexpected, the unwanted, the unnerving, that can make kindling of your life, that disaster that burns up your people and burns down your dreams?

All down the mountainside the snow's falling down around me and the massive sequoia giants, like this papery, flaky manna coming straight down. Once the people of God stood in a wilderness burning up with a scorching heat and they bore witness. Their question, *Manhue?* is Hebrew for "What is it?" And some scholars suggest the word is related to the

Egyptian word that the Israelites carried out of slavery, *manna* being related to the Egyptian word meaning "gift." What you can't explain in your life could be explained as gift.

That manna that drifted down from above, it burned up the lie of scarcity. Hadn't Jesus' own disciples suffered from scarcity: "Where can anyone get enough bread here in this desolate place to feed these people?"[36] But Jesus' mind is made of the generosity of abundance: *this is enough.*

What you have in your hand, God can always make into abundantly enough. Are we controlled by fear, driven for more, frantic for enough, suffering from scarcity? Or are we fully present to the presence of a generously abundant God? Could we look at the ashes in our churches, in our marriages, in our hopes, in our culture, and believe that in the midst of the ashes of what looks burned down, God will raise up a beautiful abundance? Because this is the startling truth: the suffering of scarcity always leads to death. But the people of God get to bring the witness of abundant manna.

When we can relax, when we can trust, when we believe there is enough to be broken and given like bread to the needy, when we can live given, as He has abundantly given to us—then we are living into the generosity of abundance. There is a more abundant, excellent bread than striving materialism, than fear-driven walls and fences and lines, than a mentality of *not-enough.*

Jesus is the Bread of Life, and you don't have to bake it or make it or fake it. Jesus is the Bread of Life and though He was rich, "yet for your sake he became poor, so that you through his poverty might become rich."[37] Culture and economics and politicians may say it takes money to make money. But Jesus' life proves it: it takes the mystery of poverty to produce the generosity of abundance; it takes what looks like ashes to make abundance.

That word in the Hebrew for abundance in Psalm 65:11: "You crown the year with your bounty, and your carts overflow with abundance," that word is *deshen*. And while it means abundant provision, "fatness," it also has another meaning—"ashes"—referring to the remains of the sacrifices on the altar where the ashes were composed of the charred remains mixed with the animals' fat.

The same Hebrew word that means abundance also means ashes. Abundance rises from ashes.

Do not ever be afraid of ashes.

They can try to burn down your hope, torch your courage, scorch your endurance, and roast your resolve, but ashes are never the last line of any of God's stories. Abundance is.

You don't have to be good enough—because He is grace abundantly enough. You don't have to be strong enough—because He is abundantly Savior enough. You don't have to be sure enough—because He is abundantly certain enough.

Abundance, not ashes, are the last line of every story of God.

I heard this afternoon that the country church around the corner was saved. Someone said that ashes were caught on the spring wind, and you could see them to the west of the steeple, all up through the spruce trees, the sky filling with all these sparking, glowing embers.

Like the rising of abundant, undeniable glory.

──────────── FOR REFLECTION ────────────

✧ Consider the brokenness and ashes in our churches, in our marriages, in our hopes, in our culture. How would you live differently today if you really believed that amid the ashes of what looks burned down, God will raise up a beautiful abundance? How are you living *deshen*—ashes being made into abundance?

✧ What would it look like to live into the mystery of abundance over the next several weeks? What choices would you make if you lived into that mystery? How are you living the truth that ashes are never the last line of God's story—abundance is?

Devotion 36

BREAKING THE DARK

"But when you give to the needy, do not let your left hand know what your right hand is doing, so that your giving may be in secret. Then your Father, who sees what is done in secret, will reward you."

MATTHEW 6:3–4

For thirty spins around the sun, these nine old nanas kept a secret from their men.

They did it in the middle of the night.

When that old ball of sun sunk down low and pulled a cover of dark up over the backside of the world, those nine nanas creaked open their back doors and made their way through the dark.

They called them "drive-bys." They did it because of MaMaw Ruth, who would send off one of her special pound cakes just to put a smile on the faces of those who had lost someone. One of the nine, Mary Ellen, said, "We started thinking about what we could do to make a difference like that. What if we had a million dollars? How would we spend it?"

They knew we're not here to make an impression; we're here to make a difference. The size of our houses, our wallets, our closets, our trophy case, and our cheerleading squad doesn't make any difference compared to the size of our hearts.

And frankly, we may be known for many things, but we will be

148

remembered by only one thing: our giving love. Anyone can have any size of heart they want. Those nine nanas came up with a list of money-saving ideas and put aside about $400 a month. "Our husbands never noticed a thing," one said.

Then they started listening—at the beauty shop and the grocer's—and when they heard about a widow or a single mother in need, guess who'd anonymously pay a utility bill or buy new clothes for the children?

They'd send a package with a note—"Somebody loves you"—and the love they sent always came with one of MaMaw Ruth's pound cakes.

In the middle of the darkest night, love is always coming for you. In the middle of the pitch-black night, those nine nanas drove slow through neighborhoods, looking for fans stuck in windows. "That told us that the people who live there? They don't have air-conditioning," Mary Ellen said. "Or we see there are no lights on at night, which means there's a good chance their utilities have been turned off. Then we return before the sun comes up, like cat burglars, and drop off a little care package."

For thirty-five years, these lovely women have been breaking the dark. Thirty-five years, nine women, 4 a.m. pitch-black, whipping up MaMaw Ruth's pound cakes and sending them all over their community. They'd open up the phone book and send pound cakes to complete strangers. Thirty-five years and hundreds of pound cakes delivered in the dead of night—*and their husbands none the wiser.*

There are those who don't need to be noticed on street corners or have their backs patted, because some people know how to shatter the dark in ways a spotlight never can. There are those who work in secret because they know real love is done in secret. There are those who don't let the right hand know what the left hand is doing because hands that move unbeknownst are best known by the Beloved.

That which is done in secret, that which is broken and given in secret, is a practicing communion.

Live Eucharist. Practice communion. Taste *koinonia.*

Mary Ellen didn't know when her husband started puzzling over the extra mileage on the car. Didn't know when he started scratching his head over withdrawals from their savings account of not-small-amounts of cash and pulled out his highlighter and started charting a path through their confounding bank statements.

Mary Ellen and those nine nanas knew they had to gather their men and fess up to what they had been up to: *an affair of the heart*.

What if the world focused on affairs of the heart instead of spending our one life on business affairs? Kiss open wounds. Caress the bruised back of the broken. Embrace suffering, because this is how you embrace the brokenhearted Christ.

And their husbands? Wanted in on the game. They wanted in on writing down addresses and anonymously paying utility bills, delivering pound cakes and pressing beauty into the world. They wanted in on the fullness of *koinonia—communion* fellowship.

Small gifts of kindness are contagious. Sometimes you want to break out of yourself and break into the sacred space of the other. And that space you seek is found when you give to the other.

The nine nanas said that. "This is our way of giving forward." Mary Ellen nodded. "We want to make sure happiness happens."

The way forward is always to give forward.

Any cake, any gift, anything anywhere can break the isolation and help someone taste the abundance of *koinonia* in the middle of the dark.

And through that love given, happiness can actually happen, and the sun will always rise.

For Reflection

✧ How could you be focused on affairs of the heart instead of spending your one life on business affairs? How are you kissing open wounds, caressing the bruised backs of the broken, embracing suffering, because this is how you embrace the brokenhearted Christ?

✧ That which is done in secret, that which is broken and given in secret, is a practicing communion. Communion is the abundant life. How are you practicing communion with Christ?

KOINONIA BROKENNESS

Therefore, I urge you, brothers and sisters, in view of God's mercy, to offer your bodies as a living sacrifice, holy and pleasing to God—this is your true and proper worship.

ROMANS 12:1

The way through brokenness is, and always has been, to break the sufferer free from the aloneness of the suffering by choosing to participate in the suffering with them—*koinonia*—choosing to stand with the suffering, stay with the suffering, and let it all be shaped into meaning that *transcends* the suffering.

My friend Elizabeth told me once, told me a dozen times, especially in the middle of the racking nights of end-stage cancer: the longer she suffered meant the more time she got to love. This is always true, everywhere. Elizabeth didn't avoid suffering, because she didn't want to avoid loving.

Because Elizabeth knew "love is the most characteristic and comprehensive act of the human being. We are most ourselves when we love; we are most the People of God when we love."[38] Loving like Jesus loves—embodying our union with Christ and our *koinonia* with the body of Christ—is the singular life work of the Jesus follower. *This is always worth the suffering.*

There is a river over which every soul must pass to reach the kingdom of heaven, and the name of that river is suffering—and the way to cross that river is a cross nailed together with love.

All who love will ultimately suffer. If we hadn't loved her, if we hadn't let her love us, our lungs wouldn't burn with this ache after we lost her. God knew when He beckoned "you shall love your neighbor" that in keeping the commandment to love, we would also keep suffering. And still He gave the command.

Love runs through us through the veins of suffering. I turn over my wrist to see that cross there again. *This is the way—the way of abundance. There is no other.*

Sometimes it's so clear: we can only love in this world if we're willing to suffer with the world. "God so suffered for the world that he gave up his only Son to suffering," wrote Nicholas Wolterstorff.[39] Suffering is at the burning core of everything because *love is.* We need not feel alone in suffering because God is a suffering God who pulls close at our call.

We can receive it if we want—there is always more God.

I had read it and never forgotten: the word *suffer* comes from the Latin "to bear under." Suffering is an act of surrender, to bear under that which is not under our control. Suffering quietly begs us to surrender so we'll win a greater wisdom, a deeper strength, a closer intimacy. Suffering says we cannot bear under this cross alone—we can only bear it if we can bear depending on others, bear the vulnerability and intimacy of *koinonia.* If we can bear depending on Him.

Elizabeth had chosen to bear under that which was beyond her control because she knew that under her were the everlasting arms of One in control. One who would never let her go. Elizabeth chose to bear under the suffering because she humbly chose to bear depending on others . . . depending on us being a community, a body, human beings who belong to each other and who will carry each other, carried by the crossbeam of the cosmos—*koinonia.*

If suffering is to bear under for each other, then wasn't that always the call? In a broken world, isn't the call always to *koinonia,* to communion with community that bears our burdens with us? Wasn't suffering then actually a call for us to be a community, to stand together and bear under, trusting that arms of abundant love are always under us?

Had I failed Elizabeth? For all my grasping justifications, had I failed living *koinonia* with her and entering into her sufferings, participating in them and in the abundance of Christ? Isn't that, after all, why we're one body? "Contribute to the needs of the saints," the apostle Paul wrote.[40] Peel open the glued eyes and see the needs as your very own because we are the same body. "Do this in remembrance of me."[41] To make Christ present, to re-member our brokenness, we must take the crushed and broken bread and swallow down our communion with a broken community.

When Elizabeth's funeral finally comes to pass, candlelight chases rising smoke in the church. Elizabeth's life lies completed, but I am unraveling it: entering each other's suffering is how to make life an abundant communion. Any shattered heart could become my shattered heart. There is no apathy in the body of Christ. Apathy is what amputates members and limbs of the body. There is no distance in the body of Christ—it's distance and indifference that dismember the body, and we are all desperate to stop feeling abandoned and cut off. This is the reality of the body of Christ: selfishness is a form of self-mutilation.

We are all a body. We belong to one another. We are one. This is the practical reality. Relationship is the only real reality. Unless our everyday reality reflects the practical reality of our oneness, we live a horror story of distortion and dis-memberment. To be the re-membering people—this is the work of those living a meaningful, abundant life in a brokenhearted world.

I look up in the church, look up at Elizabeth's funeral, and the moment is weightless, lifted in a spiral of candle flame underneath the big cross on the wall. *Do this, all of life, in re-membrance of Me.*

FOR REFLECTION

✧ How have you been avoiding brokenness and suffering—which has led to avoiding loving?

✧ How are you embracing the daily call to *koinonia*, to communion with community that bears our burdens with us, trusting that His arms of abundant love are always under you?

Devotion 38

YADAH ABUNDANCE

*It is a good thing to give thanks [yadah] unto the LORD, and
to sing praises unto thy name, O Most High.*

PSALM 92:1 KJV

W hatever."
        The Wednesday morning before folks eat turkey and pie and
browse the Black Friday flyers, I wake up to this smothering of fog and
this teen muttering it through the kitchen: *"Whatever."*

And what do you do but say that's not quite the way to start off the
day, and he shrugs his shoulders and slams the bathroom door behind
him, and I get it.

It's there on the mantel, this framed God-thunder: "Give Thanks." It's
no neon sign, more this painting in a quaint Shaker style. There are only
two remaining Shakers now. I think about that.

Think about whether they're still giving thanks and if this whole
Pilgrim Thanksgiving thing, this whole holiday shebang, isn't a bit of
quaint antiquated denial in a world that's right busted and hemorrhaging
a mess straight out the side.

Because there are angry airwaves about a whole world of broken
division, there are headlines about school-aged children being killed and
bombs falling and heated politics and polarized, frustrated Facebook
streams, and I sat with a mother who stood over a hole in the earth and

watched as they laid her son in soil and they just buried her baby in dirt and expected her to walk away.

I'm looking this mama in the eye and I want to claw the damp, clammy earth open with my very fingernails and who cares how many days Jesus stayed away from Bethany after Lazarus died—why does He not come here, *here*, and resurrect our cold joy?

Who doesn't watch the news and just howl? Who doesn't breathe through wounds and grieve for what was or dreamed and isn't? How do you sit around a table and bow your head in thanks when parts of this world and bits of you are somewhere busted and broken?

And I peel squash and there is God and there is all the debate and pain and news everywhere and *yada, yada, yada.*

Yadah, it's Hebrew, and it literally means to hold out the hand. There are so many ways to hold out our hands these days in the midst of all kinds of brokenness:

- ✧ to bemoan with a wringing of hands
- ✧ to confess with open hands
- ✧ to revere with an extending of hands
- ✧ to raise hands in giving thanks

Yadah—it is the whisper of Psalm 92:1. And it is a good thing to *yadah* around the holiday tables, to wring our hands and shake our heads and bemoan sin and suffering and injustice. To confess where we have failed, our hands open in helplessness.

It is a good thing to *yadah* around the tables—to revere the God who made us all by extending a hand when arms are stubbornly folded. It is a good thing to *yadah* around the tables—in the midst of rising voices, to raise a hand and give thanks, to brazenly confess that God is deeply good though the world is desperately not.

And you can hear it now at the cusp of the feasting, the *yadah, yadah,*

yadah, that sings relentless and bold: we won't stop confessing He is good and we won't stop thanking Him for grace and we won't stop holding out our hands—and taking His hand.

We won't stop believing that *God is good* is not some trite quip for the good days but a radical defiant cry for the terrible days.

That *God is good* is not a stale one-liner when all's happy but a saving *lifeline* when all's hard.

And we will keep giving thanks, *yadah, yadah, yadah*, because giving thanks is only this: making the canyon of pain into a megaphone to proclaim the ultimate goodness of God.

I'm holding the squash in hand. That's what the mother had said standing there in her tsunami of grief: "I believe God is good. *I believe that is all there really is.*"

And every time I give thanks, I confess to the universe the goodness of God. I had touched her hand. She had said it, her eyes so clear, like you could see straight into her, into all that remains.

The morning fog ebbs across harvested fields. Thanksgiving in all things accepts the deep mystery of God through everything. We give thanks to God not because of how we feel but because of *who He is*.

No amount of regret changes the past, no amount of anxiety changes the future, but any amount of gratitude changes the present. In the stressful times, seek God. In the painful times, praise God. In the terrible times, trust God. And at all times, *thank God*.

There will be bowed heads around all the tables. There will be lights flickering brave to burn back the brokenness and dark, and there will be a believing in relentless redemption and a reaching out and all these hands reaching around and out through the brokenness and there will be *yadah, yadah, yadah* all around the tables, this steady confessing of the abundant goodness of God—of thanking Him come whatever.

There are leaves fallen frosted across the lawn, and there's a way that bravely shimmers on.

For Reflection

- ✧ Since giving thanks is only making the canyon of brokenness into a megaphone to proclaim the abundant goodness of God, can you recall five things to be grateful for in the midst of hard, broken places you've experienced?

- ✧ How can you choose, through the brokenness, to continually speak *yadah, yadah, yadah,* this steady confessing of the abundant goodness of God—of thanking Him come whatever? What can you practically commit to?

Devotion 39

BEARING BURDENS

"Watch and pray so that you will not fall into temptation.
The spirit is willing, but the flesh is weak."

MATTHEW 26:41

There is a two-inch hoarfrost of lacy ice coating every reaching limb in the woods the morning the Farmer and I sit and watch the documentary *The Forger* again.

There are gauzy grey clouds listing low on the edge of the fields, like the woods exhaled, relieved. The Forger is ninety-one years old. His long white hair is its own cloud of mystery, of secrets of his own.

As a young kid working at a dye shop, the man who eventually became known as the Forger became obsessed with the chemistry of colorants, inks, dyes. Soon his entire life was one of ink and papers and secrets, of forging food ration papers for Jewish children, creating passports to save families during World War II.

His voice quavers now as he talks from behind the haze of his white beard, talks of how he did what he did. "I had to stay awake as long as possible. Fight against sleep. The math was simple. In one hour, I made thirty fake documents. If I slept for one hour, thirty people would die."

Stay awake as long as possible. Fight against sleep.

During World War II, the Forger, who took not one penny for his efforts, saved more than 14,000 lives.

160

"All humans are equal, whatever their origins, their beliefs, their skin color." His voice cracks. "There are no superiors, no inferiors. That is not acceptable for me."

In that moment, I thought he had said everything.

All humans are equal—because all are equally made by God.

In his famous sermon "The American Dream," Martin Luther King Jr. said:

> The whole concept of the *imago dei* . . . the "image of God," is the idea that all men have something within them that God injected . . . And this gives him a uniqueness, it gives him worth, it gives him dignity. And we must never forget this as a nation: there are no gradations in the image of God. Every man from a treble white to a bass black is significant on God's keyboard, precisely because every man is made in the image of God. One day we will learn that. We will know one day that God made us to live together as brothers and to respect the dignity and worth of every man.[42]

We will never reflect the image of Christ to the world unless we see the image of God in everyone. We're created to only be truly strong *when we all live like we all belong.*

The Forger who spent his life giving so that others might have life, he looked past everything, seemed to say it to everyone, to the universe, to himself: "If I hadn't been able to do anything, I wouldn't have been able to bear it."

If I hadn't been able to do something to help bear others' burdens, I wouldn't have been able to bear living.

Unless we battle injustice, stand for the outsider, the oppressed, imagine ourselves in the place of the displaced, risk our lives so others can have life, we can't genuinely bear the grace in our own lives—*because the grace we've been given, it's always meant to be given.*

Unless you give forward the abundant grace you've been given—you won't be able to bear the abundant grace of your own life. You won't be able to bear the grace of your own life, unless you come bearing grace and hope and justice and kindness and life and joy *to everyone in your life.*

Your life breaks in the deepest ways—unless you lighten your soul by giving forward some of the grace you've been given to lighten someone else's load.

Stay awake. Fight against sleep, against distraction, against apathy, despair, privilege, cynicism, indifference.

The woods, the beckoning fields, the world—all ring with the words of Martin Luther King Jr., whose words but echo the King of Kings: "Life's most persistent and urgent question is, 'What are you doing for others?'"[43]

And there's an answer that lives cruciform, broken and given like bread, a broken way forward through brokenness, that gives grace forward, that gives forward, that chooses to make its life about being a gift, that moves dreams and hopes and abundant wholeness forward.

In the midst of deep brokenness across a struggling world, there are truths that run deeper and more certain than those of the whole rooted woods: we won't be able to really bear living unless we really bear each other's burdens.

At the edge of the woods, you could see the low-lying clouds rising, *always rising,* the reaching limbs breaking free of the winter frost with this determined, lifting grace.

FOR REFLECTION

- ✧ Your life breaks in the deepest ways—unless you lighten your soul by giving forward some of the grace you've been given to lighten someone else's load. How are you doing (or not doing) that?
- ✧ Sit with the deep meaningfulness of what the abundant life looks like: "If I hadn't been able to do something to help bear others' burdens, I wouldn't have been able to bear living." How is God moving you to respond?

TRAMPLING CHRIST

"Therefore everyone who confesses Me before men, I will also confess him before My Father who is in heaven. But whoever denies Me before men, I will also deny him before My Father who is in heaven."

MATTHEW 10:32–33 NASB

The administration wanted him to trample on Christ.

The Japanese officials wanted the Christian to deny Christ, to take the sole of his foot and press it into the image of Christ, a copper cast of his Savior pressed into the dirt, what the Japanese called the *fumi-e.*

"Trample. Go ahead—trample on Him."

Over and over again, the Japanese officials urged the Christian to deny his God and walk all over Him.

What would I do? I look away from the movie screen, hardly able to stand the question—the torturing of my own soul. I sit in a hushed and gutted theatre, two of my sons leaning forward with me—and you could hear their ticking gears of courage: there is always a way to walk forward that doesn't trample Christ.

One of our boys turns to me, leans close, and whispers, "There is nothing that can happen in the public square that can shake the private convictions of the heart."

My wrestling quietly, momentarily, stills. Maybe—no laws of the state can make you an apostate of your beliefs.

I have no idea how many of us stepped across their threshold, the threshold of our Syrian newcomer family from Aleppo, who for several years were fleeing refugees. But there we all were, in their living room with babies slung on hips of laughing mamas and worn farmers with hands stuffed into old Wranglers, a bunch of far-flung neighbors circled up in that crowded living room, like hope can actually move right into wherever you are and set up house.

Marlene's was the first voice to rise above the din. "I've got to say, of everything I've ever done, getting to know you as a family, and helping you rebuild your lives, has been one of the greatest experiences of my life." She smiles over at Zaccharias and Fatin.

And God commanded, "The foreigner residing among you must be treated as your native-born. Love them as yourself, for you were foreigners in Egypt. I am the LORD your God."[44]

"Thank you for letting us just . . . be your friends. And this, this is what friends do." Marlene makes a sweeping gesture around the crowded room. She's found them a doctor and taken them in for checkups, dentist appointments, eye exams.

"No stranger had to spend the night in the street, for my door was always open to the traveler," Job said.[45] The art of really living is giving, and our theology is best expressed in the willingness of our hospitality.

Oh, dear God, how do I live with heart and hands and door open to the stranger?

My sister chokes up. "Fatin?" Fatin looks up, her little boy Mohamad on her lap.

"You're like family to us," my sister enunciates the words slowly, clearly, hoping Fatin's growing English can understand. My sister leans over a stove every day with Fatin. Practices English with her every day. "And I . . . I can't imagine our lives without you." She reaches out her hand to Fatin.

Fatin tucks back her white hijab, leans forward, like she's trying to catch her heart before it breaks, but she's too late and her heart's streaming liquid down her face.

And Fatin is Ruth, overcome by Boaz's kindness: "She dropped to her knees, then bowed her face to the ground. 'How does this happen that you should pick me out and treat me so kindly—*me*, a foreigner?'"[46]

"Thank you. Just—thank you." Fatin looks up, all her love and thanks and tears streaming down, and I try to hold her gaze, but everything's swimming a bit with pieces of my heart. "Everything, for all the things. Thank you."

The Farmer, who's led us all, who's sitting beside Zach like he does nearly every day, he nods, he and I both brimming. I know what he's thinking: *If I hadn't been able to do anything, I wouldn't have been able to bear it.*

I look into Fatin's and Zaccharias's faces—and they bear the image of God. They have survived the bombing hell of Aleppo, they have snatched their children from an imploding, crumbling world of blood-hunting bombs and decapitations and starvation, they have fled the mouth of the ravenous monster that once was their home, and they carry the image of God.

We will never reflect the image of Christ to the world unless we first see the image of God in everyone. Sitting there, thinking that our Fatin could be buried under the rubble of Aleppo, that her three-year-old Mohamad could be bloodied and orphaned and eating grass, I had never known it quite like I did in that moment: there are a thousand ways to deny Christ.

There are a thousand ways to trample on the image of Christ, to walk through the world and deny the words of Christ, the ways of Christ, the welcome of Christ.

Do I trample on Christ when I am more about protecting my way of life than protecting others' very life? Is the way I'm walking every day trampling on Christ all the time?

"Sin is for one man to walk brutally over the life of another and to be quite oblivious of the wounds he has left behind."[47]

I feel more than a bit undone. I feel as nauseated as I did sitting watching that movie *Silence*, watching officials implore believers to step on the image of God. *No forces in any era can force us to trample the image of God in the world.*

The only way to not trample on Christ in the world is to not trample on the marginalized, oppressed, and voiceless in the world. If my life denies that I am about the oppressed and crushed—my life denies the gospel and Christ.

I feel small in a small room in a small corner of the world, and a small little boy from Aleppo reaches his hand up, slides his fingers through mine.

And a whole world of people will decide who Jesus is—by who we are.

Little Mohamad looks up at me. And I look into his eyes.

When we turn our backs on the fleeing, we turn our backs on Christ.

What if—Jesus comes in the disguise of the desperate refugee, and to refuse Him is to refuse one's identity as a Christian?

And the words echo: "Lord, when did we see you hungry or thirsty or a stranger or needing clothes or sick or in prison, and did not help you?"[48]

I lean over and scoop up little Mohamad, whose young life has known the tortures of war, and he puts his arms around my neck and now is the time to welcome Christ.

There can be more compassion in our hearts than fear in the world, and now is the time to care for Christ.

Mohamad's sisters gather round for hugs too and we hold on to each other and now is the time to protect Christ, advocate for Christ, risk for Christ.

There is the heart of God beating clearly in the silence, like a begging prayer pounding loud in my veins, my ears:

Because if you walk brutally over the life of another, if you trample Christ, reject Christ, deny Christ, then who will pray for your tortured souls?

I don't know how long I sit there that night with little Mohamad, watching him play, watching his little feet circle the room.

I don't know how long I have felt this—this growing, abundant hope, that there is always a way to walk forward that doesn't trample Christ who walks all around you.

FOR REFLECTION

✧ Who in a broken world do you see being trampled? How can you resolutely and practically honor the image of God in them this week?

✧ What would living given into an abundant communion with Christ look like for you right now, as you walk through your day with various people? How is the cruciform Christ calling you forward?

Part Five

How Can the Brokenhearted Release Control?

Devotion 41

ABUNDANT FRUIT

When they hurled their insults at him, he did not retaliate;
when he suffered, he made no threats. Instead, he entrusted
himself to him who judges justly.

1 PETER 2:23

I meet this farmer, Daoud, with beat-up hands, nine miles southwest of Bethlehem. He asks what I do. I tell him I'm a farmer's wife, daughter of a farmer, granddaughter of a farmer—yeah, farmers are about the only thing our family tree has ever known (well, that, and a whole mess of ridiculously crazy kids).

To get here, I had to push through this herd of goats straggling down the road. Meanwhile, there are clashes in Jerusalem and suicide bombers ripping through children in Iraq.

Daoud has this rock at the gate to his farm inscribed with the words "we refuse to be enemies." He kneels down and digs in fruit trees to replace the hundreds that were cut down and buried in the dark by the nameless. I wonder if he tries to imagine their faces.

How do you grow in grace and not in resentment?

The farmer moves his hands quietly when he talks, like he can cut through the air, cut through all the dung and get down to truth. His voice is low and gentle and slow. His fruit trees now cut down, his water and electricity long shut off, but he has all the deeds to his land. "All we want is to just stay on our land. My grandfather didn't want to just live in the village and work the land like all his neighbors. He dreamed of his children growing up with the land always under their feet."

And I nod slow hearing the reverberating in the marrow. There is nothing like the land we come from, and we will return to it for food we grew out of its dust, and we will return to it as dust and it's like our kin. And until we realize and come to peace with that, we live in conflict with what abundant living is.

The word *humility* comes from *humus*, the earth. It's only knowing you came from this humble dirt that you can bear any honest fruit.

When Daoud tells me they won't ever leave their land, I catch his eye. My dad always said there was a lot he may love, but his land was sacred. Selling away your land was like selling your soul. "You understand?" Daoud asks. "We cannot leave our land . . . and we cannot have enemies."

Our eyes don't leave each other—we all belong to each other and to this dirt—and what happens next rips through my rib cage with the force of God. The light catches his eye and grows into this blazing grace, and I know: the only thing that can overcome evil is good. Returning evil with evil—*just overcomes us.*

Being enemies is not an option. Being human beings belonging to each other is the only option. And it doesn't make one iota of difference if you're living in the middle of global war zones or some battle zone in your own community or inside yourself—you can wage conflict over the injustice, or you can plow the pain into purpose.

Farmer Daoud had grabbed that plow. "We take all our frustrations over injustices and we drill them into soil to grow incredible possibilities."

Channel negativity into creativity.

And don't pick a side. Pick a person—the Person of Jesus. And go pick His ways.

Where there's conflict—we don't have to condemn the other, we don't have to curse the future, we don't have to circumvent the circumstances.

Where there's conflict, there's an opportunity—to practice being like Christ.

The world would change if, like Jesus, we chose:

a donkey over a steed,
a cross over a crown,
a palm branch over bitterness,
and abundant grace over any guilt.

Jesus walked this same land of Farmer Daoud, and He'd turned and He cursed a fruit tree because it was nothing but a non-fruit-producing fraud. I'd scrawled that across a journal with this dying, splotchy pen: Are our lives bearing fruit—or are we duct-taping on fruit to impress others with our lives?

"I'm telling you to love your enemies," Jesus said. "Let them bring out the best in you, not the worst."[49] Let your enemies bring out the best in you, the abundant fruit in you. The abundance of Christ's love, Christ's mercy, Christ's grace, Christ's givenness in you.

When the sun set over the fields of Daoud's fruit trees, you could see Jerusalem where Jesus had walked through the crowds that were against Him. And you could hear the goats far off to the west.

FOR REFLECTION

✧ How are taking all your brokenhearted frustrations with people and letting them break you open to grow abundant change? How are you channeling negativity into creativity? How is your life bearing abundant fruit—and where are you duct-taping on fruit to impress others?

✧ How are you refusing to be enemies, letting your enemies, hard people in your life, bring out the best in you, the abundant fruit of Christ in you? What would it look like today, this week, to let them bring out the best in you—the abundance of Christ in you?

173

Devotion 42

DAILY REPENTANCE

Repent, then, and turn to God, so that your sins may be wiped out, that times of refreshing may come from the Lord.
ACTS 3:19

When he sits down on the stool for his last haircut before driving away from here for the last time as a boy, I'm a bit desperate to somehow turn the last time around to the first time again.

"Well?"

"Short, Mom," he says, sitting in the chair, and I can still see that scar on the side of his head where he fell when he was two. *How is he so tall in this chair?* "Just cut it short."

The years were short, Son. The years can be too short, and all the ways you fell short, too long. The hair clippers slip up the bare nape of his neck. I cut slowly . . . everything falling away.

Do I apologize one more time for all I got wrong? There is always enough time to ask for enough forgiveness and grace.

Then out of the blue, he says it under the hum of the clippers: "Just— thanks for everything, Mom. Couldn't have been a better mom. All the books you read to us. All the walks through the woods. And making me keep practicing piano. And saying sorry. Thanks for always saying sorry."

Trim along the nape of his neck. Fight back this burning ember in my throat. There is only so much time.

But I got so much wrong.

After seventeen years, there it is: I have been the broken mama who punished when I needed to pray. Who hollered at kids when I needed to help. Who lunged forward when I should have fallen back on Jesus. Until you see the depths of brokenness in you, you can't know the depths of Christ's love for you. Joshua's hair feels like water slipping through fingers.

There are dishes stacked on the counter like memories tonight, and there are kids sprawled across the front-porch swing trying to read the same book at the same time. And there's me cutting our son's hair one last time before he drives away from here. And for crying out loud, there is only so much time to be broken and given and multiplied.

I never expected to get so much wrong. I never expected love like this. I never expected so much joy. *Be patient with God's patient work in you.*

"What does Gram always say?" He asks me quiet, his head bowed so his neck looks like an offering before the shearers. Yeah, if my mama's said it to me once, she's said it to me and the kids a thousand times. "It's not that you aren't going to get it wrong; it's what you do with it afterward."

It's not that your heart isn't going to break; it's how you let the brokenness be made into abundance afterward.

And afterward, I'd had to say sorry—no, I *got to* say sorry—so many times.

Isn't repentance a foundational thesis of life, of taking the broken way of abundance?

Martin Luther's first thesis of the ninety-five was "When our Lord and Master Jesus Christ said, 'Repent,' he willed the entire life of believers to be one of repentance."[50] If the whole life of believers should be repentance, then what is the call of the whole life of believers but a broken way? Reduce repentance to a single act at the beginning of your Christian life and you reduce your entire Christian life to an act. An act of pretending, a sham act of posturing, a feigning act of pretense.

One night, I'd taken that same pen I used to both write down the *eucharisteo* for endless gifts and the *koinonia* of that cross on my wrist, and I'd broke down, written page after page of repentance, of every sin I could think of that I had committed. What I had been tempted by, what I had done that no one had ever known. The day I whacked a kid hard and the thousand different ways I'd cheated me and God and us and them in countless ways, all the times I spit out toxic words and scorched hearts I'd claimed I loved but I had loved me more. Pages and pages stained with my bloody hands.

Repent. You are broken and you don't have to pretend you are not. What a relief. *Repent.* It's the very first word of Jesus' teaching—not love, not grace; the very first word of the gospel is repent.[51] You begin to break your brokenness when you break down with your brokenness—when you hand it over to the One broken for you.

If repentance isn't a daily part of your life, how is grace a daily part of your life?

Repentance is what keeps turning you around, around, sanding you down, re-forming you, remaking you—making you abundantly real.

I cut away stray hairs over his ears.

Sorry. For all the Monopoly games I didn't play while there was still time. Sorry for not saying yes more at the right time and for saying no at the wrong times, and sorry for flying off the handle and for not flying more kites, sorry for not being more passionate, not being more willing to suffer for love of you. Outloving is the only medicine that healed anything.

There is still light. All across the wheat fields, there is still light.

- ✧ It's all okay: *Repent.* You are broken and you don't have to pretend you are not. What a relief! What could you repent of to deepen that abundant relief?
- ✧ How is repentance a continual, foundational thesis of your life, of your daily choosing the broken way of abundance? How is God convicting you right now?

Devotion 43

FOR THE GOOD

*And we know that in all things God works for the good of those
who love him, who have been called according to his purpose.*

ROMANS 8:28

When that window shattered into seven billion pieces, a sliver stuck my heart—and maybe a sliver is all we ever have?

It wasn't so much that our farm boy had turned the tractor too sharp, or backed the tractor into the auger, or even that the full window of the tractor had exploded all over him, the tractor cab, the yard. It was the way he turned away to hide what was slipping down all stinging wet, him more broken than any glass.

He brushed his lap, then the tears, and then drove the tractor back out to the field to fill up with his next load of wheat.

Did he know that when we battle onward even when we're broken, all the fixing comes in the moving forward?

When the Farmer looks up from the combine to his boy, he nods quiet and the farm boy turns his eyes away.

Is it too painful to face love squarely when we're ashamed?

I crawl up in the combine cab, sit down beside the Farmer. The Farmer hits the button, and the combine auger begins to unload into the farm boy's wagon.

"What do we do?" I hardly murmur above the roar of the combine.

My hands twist in my lap. He senses my words more than hears them. He knows I don't mean the window. I can't look away from our son bent over that tractor steering wheel.

"You know how it is, Ann . . ." The Farmer glances at the wagon, our son driving alongside. "From where we stand, we can't see whether something's good or bad. All we see is God is sovereign and always good, working all things for good."

The wheat's bowed before the combine. "The window's gone and the cab's dented. And sure, he's shook up and there's the cost . . . but do we know these are bad things?" He focused on the wheat that's lying down before the combine. "You know that story you told me years ago, the story of the white horse? I think this is another hour of the white horse."

I'd written it down when I first heard it from Max Lucado, an old story from South America.[52] What I remembered of it was how a white steed appeared in the paddocks of an old man and how all the villagers had congratulated him on such good fortune. When the horse disappeared one day from the stable, the townsfolk were convinced it was a curse.

The old man only offered, "Whether it be a curse or a blessing, I can't say. All we can see is a fragment. Who can say what will come next?" This man lived surrendered to the will of God alone: "I cannot see as He sees."

When the horse returned about two weeks later with a dozen more horses, the townsfolk declared it a blessing, yet the old man said only, "I give thanks for His will."

When the man's only son was thrown from the white steed and broke both legs, the town bemoaned the curse of the white horse. But the old man only offered, *It is as He wills and I give thanks for His will.*

When a war draft took all the young men but the son with the broken legs, the villagers praised the white horse again, but the old man said, "We see only a sliver of the sum. No one is wise enough to know. Only God knows. We cannot see how the bad might be good. God is sovereign and He is good. And He works all things together for good."

Hasn't the lie since our beginning been that we can know? Satan hissed that we'd know good and evil, that we'd really see. But the father of lies, he duped us. Though we ate of that tree we did not become like God. We have no knowledge apart from God. Our heart optics are not omniscient. Our focus need only be on Him, to faithfully see His Word, and to wholly obey. Therein is the abundant tree of life.

The Farmer slows toward the end of the field, turns off the combine auger, and the farm boy nods to his dad through the window that broke— *but who are we to see?* The son pulls his full wagon to unload at the grain bin.

"Yes, it's a white horse hour." The Farmer turns on the headland, pulls back into the field, and looks up at the farm boy headed toward the bin. "A boy came to the field today. But I think we may be bringing home a man. God's up to good."

I reach over and lay my hand on his knee. All we can see is Christ. And in Him all is being made into abundant grace.

And in the combine's rearview mirror, I see only what we can always see—just a sliver of the whole, swaying behind us in a whisper of wind.

FOR REFLECTION

✧ How would it change how you view current brokenness around you if you thought of it as but a sliver, and God is working through it for abundant good?

✧ What if your response to incidents today was "white horse thinking": *It is as He wills and I give thanks for His will.* Would you take that dare to more fully experience an abundance of His peace, joy, and goodness?

Devotion 44

ABUNDANTLY OKAY

"What do you think? If a man owns a hundred sheep, and one of them wanders away, will he not leave the ninety-nine on the hills and go to look for the one that wandered off?"

MATTHEW 18:12

You can look up at the calendar today and exhale: It's okay to feel bone tired—you have One who gives His bone and His body for you and beckoned, *Come rest.*

It's okay to feel disillusioned—you have One who destroys cheap illusions of perfection and offers you His. It's okay to feel done—you have One who listens to the last nail be driven in and proclaims all the hellish things finished. It's okay to feel battered and bruised—you have One who storms your battles, takes back everything that needs a comeback, and proves His side won. It's okay to feel a bit like a fool—you have One who proves that real love always makes anyone the wisest fool who gives more, lives more, forgives more, because love defies logic, because love is the self-giving, cruciform foolishness that is the ultimate wisdom of the universe.

It's okay to feel behind—you have One who is the Head and the Author and the Maker and the Finisher and the Carrier and the Warrior, and nothing is over until He carries you over the finish line.

It's okay to feel on the outside—you have One who is passionate about you on the inside, who wants to be with you so desperately, He moves into you, gets into your skin, so you're never alone, dwells in you, moves into your empty places, your rejected places, your abandoned places, and fills you with chosenness and wholeness and with-ness . . . because He knows the fulfilled life is an inside job.

It's okay to feel spent—you have One who pays you all His attention, who says you are worth costing Him everything. And then He bought you back from the pit because you are priceless to Him.

It's okay to feel whatever you feel because you don't judge your feelings; you feel your feelings—and then give them to God. Feelings are meant be fully felt and then fully surrendered to God.

It's okay to not feel okay because you have One who made you His one. You have One who left the clamor of the ninety-nine, to find you, remind you, remake you, rename you, release you. You have One who is more ready to forgive what you've done than you are to forget; One who is more ready to give you grace than you are to give up; One who is more than ready to always stand with you than you are to run. One who is a greater Lover, Rescuer, Savior, Friend than you have ever imagined Him to be even when your love for Him is most on fire.

This week, these worries, this world, may leave you feeling a bit depressed, but you have a God who is obsessed with you. His love for you is oceanic, His welcome of you is enthusiastic, His purpose through you is cosmic, His commitment to you is astronomic, and His hope in you is meteoric.

It's beautiful how that goes: whatever the story is today, it's abundantly okay. Because we know the ending and how it will be the beginning of the truest happily ever after.

Whatever the story is today, it's abundantly okay. Because the Writer of the story has written Himself into the hardest places of yours and is softening the edges of everything with redeeming grace.

✧ Where do you feel the sharp edge of brokenness in your life right now? How is God comforting you that it is abundantly okay?

✧ Sit with the abundant grace that His love for you is oceanic, His welcome of you is enthusiastic, His purpose through you is cosmic, His commitment to you is astronomic, and His hope in you is meteoric. What do you want to express to God right now about the abundance that He envelops you in?

Devotion 45

ABUNDANTLY AMAZING

Rend your heart and not your garments. Return to the LORD
your God, for he is gracious and compassionate.

JOEL 2:13

We're not that far into Lent and forget that sign of dust they brush on the center of your forehead. I'm bowed over the sink after a teenage daughter slammed out the back door. Slammed out of my ugly diatribe.

And I'm thinking I need something more direct, right there on the middle of the brow. Like the *L* sign. The one the Farmer frowns deep at me and shakes his head that it isn't true.

She says she didn't. I say she did. I don't know how it suddenly got so loud and we both lost. I do know there are parenting days when the terms of endearment can get confusing and it all feels more like *the terms of endurement.*

Our arguing, it can go in circles. I don't like it. What I like even less somedays is me. It's there in the center of the kitchen table, the wooden Lenten wreath—the figurine of Christ carrying His cross, encircling round everything on His way to Calvary.

Encircle our crazy circles, Lord?

Everything blurs and spills. Whoever had the crazy idea that Lent was for the good who were forsaking some lush little luxury? Lent's for the messes, the mourners, the muddled—for the people right lost. Lent's

184

not about making anybody acceptable to a Savior—but about making everybody aware of why they need a Savior.

Wasn't it C. S. Lewis who said we are to be little Christs?[53]

If I'm following Him on His way to Golgotha, the place of the skull . . . I finger the figurine of Christ carrying the cross.

Lent's about little dyings.

How could so much of my flesh still be alive?

The girl whose side the sharp edge of my tongue pierced, she's escaped to under the Manitoba maple tree. She's leaning up against the trunk's mark—the scar mark where a windstorm ripped off a limb last spring.

How could I have said those things and what part of this glorious child has my storm ripped off and how have words left marks?

In one wild moment, my disordered desires can betray how quickly I can lose my God-orientation. "Who will rescue me from this body that is subject to death?"[54] I'm this spring rain over sin and everything swims.

Encircle us, Christ, in all our dizzying chaos. When I feel like I'm drowning, I'm at last ready to drown in the ocean of God's unearned grace.

The sun sets. She's at the couch, cheek against the window, looking out. I sit softly beside her, say it softer . . .

"I'm sorry." I reach out and her shoulder's warm under my hand. This way of somehow holding her, healing her. I murmur it again and again, trying to find the way out, the way back, and repentance is always the first step. "I sinned and I'm so sorry; *I'm so sorry.*"

Hadn't Mama always said that: "It's not that you aren't going to blow it. It's what you do with it after."

"I'm the one who did it wrong, Mama." She turns from the window, turns to face me.

She hardly whispers it, but it reverberates loud in this canyon, *"Sorry, Mama."* And everything fills and our eyes find each other, flow into each other, and I reach for her hand, squeeze her hand, and forgiveness is a river that sweeps everything away.

"You know what you are?" I smile into her eyes searching mine.

She shakes her head, eyes brimming.

That's when I know she needs a sign of who she is, right there on her forehead. That's when I know she needs to know who she is, no matter what is said, what happens, what storm descends. *She and I both.* Her mother too needs to make new signs to hang everywhere, to live under.

"You know that index and the thumb that makes the *L* sign—the loser sign?" She half grins. She knows what her father thinks of me making that hand gesture and she says it slow, "Yeeees?"

"See how these fingers can angle—how they can bend in surrender to Him. And if you lay the other index finger across, pick up your cross, and follow Him—there it is—there's the sign to wear, the sign showing the way out of a mess: *A*—abundantly *amazing.*"

She has to know this, that the word *maze*, it comes from the act of wandering in a maze. The word *amaze* comes from being bewildered, overwhelmed with wonder, *maze.* The losers, the ones lost in the labyrinth of life, lost wandering in the maze of life, are the ones made amazing *by the One who solves the mazes of life.*

I touch her cheek. "In Him, you're already amazing."

She blushes and I laugh, nod my head yes, insisting to this daughter who has to know her Father's heart for her now because of the Son.

In the flesh, you're a mess. In Christ, you amaze. *Get. That. In.*

I sign the *A* over her, and Christ with the scars, He marks her. *"You're amazing."*

"And you are too, Mama."

She laughs and when I give myself the *L* sign, she reaches over and turns it into an *A* and I brim with tears.

And all the daughters, we could do that for each other, turn all the *L*'s into *A*'s, and we could wear the sign of the Son and *know it is true*: you don't need higher self-esteem; you need greater self-grace that comes from the depths of His grace. Amazing grace in your self-talk makes everything amazing.

The wooden Lent wreath is there on the table. And it all comes round like a circle—His grace that you accept for yourself is the same grace you then extend to others, which then graciously circles back to you.

And there too, the figurine of Christ, there on the circling wreath, there with the sign of sacrifice, showing how to move through Lent. How to move in the right direction, encircling the maze and the mess with this already abundantly amazing grace.

FOR REFLECTION

✧ Where are there places in your heart where God is wanting right now to touch your unspoken broken with His tender, amazing grace?

✧ How is God asking you today to extend the abundant forgiveness and amazing grace He has given to you to others who may have wounded you?

Devotion 46

BROKERS OF HEALING

*But he was pierced for our transgressions, he was crushed
for our iniquities; the punishment that brought us peace was
on him, and by his wounds we are healed.*

ISAIAH 53:5

There's a chip in the handle of this teacup. I feel like I'm seeing everything for the first time.

I could have *koinonia* here. I could have communion with Christ; I could
share in the sufferings of Christ, not only by caring for others in their suffering,
but also by coming to Christ with my own. We could woo God by caring for
all the wounds . . . and Christ in us can heal them all. It's all wholly Him,
His broken way. The brave baring of all the broken in their brokenness can
offer the miracle of communion. *Never be afraid of being a broken thing.*

He's inviting me to heal, but also to see my most meaningful calling: to
be His healing to the hurting. My own brokenness, driving me into Christ's,
is exactly where I can touch the brokenhearted. Our most meaningful
purpose can be found exactly in our most painful brokenness. I'm not sure
I'd known: *we can be brokers of healing exactly where we have known
the most brokenness.*

Why have we swallowed the lie that we can only help if we're perfect?
The cosmic truth sealed in the wounds of the broken God is that the greatest
brokers of abundance know an unspoken broken. Wrapping my hands

around the empty, cracked mug feels like this strange comfort. *It's all going to be okay.* What makes us feel the most disqualified for the abundant life is actually what makes us the most qualified. It's the broken and the limping, the wounded and the scarred, the stragglers and the strugglers, who may know best where to run with wounds. It's only the broken who know where the cracks are and how our broken wounds can be the very thin places that reveal God . . . and allow us to feel His safe holding hand.

Those who've known an unspoken broken can speak the most real healing. Stay weak and dependent. This is how you stay strong in God.

The morning after the detour in the woods, that mother-daughter mess sorted out under the maple trees, the girl finds me at the stove with an empty pot in hand and she lays her head on my shoulder and she whispers, "Mama? Yesterday? When you listened . . . I felt loved. When you owned things . . . I didn't feel so alone. Just—when you let my heart say everything—and you weren't afraid? . . . I felt close."

And I'd closed my eyes and let it come. Reached out to touch her cheek right there on my shoulder.

Maybe—safety is where the brokenness of two hearts meet. Maybe there are these "'patches of Godlight' in the woods of our experience," like C. S. Lewis wrote.[55]

And maybe there can be a thousand ways out of the wilderness of our wounds.

FOR REFLECTION

✧ How is God working through your own brokenness to step into and touch the broken hearts of others? How might He be calling you forward?

✧ What are the broken places you need to bravely own today, to experience more of an abundant communion with Christ?

Devotion 47

PALMS OPEN WIDE

Who is wise and understanding among you? Let them show it by their good life, by deeds done in the humility that comes from wisdom.

JAMES 3:13

So my grandma Ruth, she told me if you found a man who'd weep over a story, that was a man you could marry.

The morning of Palm Sunday, the porridge boils over and burns on the stove. A girl here tries on three dresses, slumps into the kitchen, and declares she has nothing to wear. A younger girl here can't find her something for her hair—only this mangled bow one that's missing the barrette. Caleb points out that someone's dropped their orange peels all down the back garage steps.

I'm strangling down a frustrated rant.

Malakai, reaching for milk for his porridge, slips off his chair and splits his lip right open on the edge of the table. There is blood dripping on our kitchen floor on Palm Sunday—for real.

And on the kitchen table, there's that bent silhouette of Christ carrying a cross. He's nearing the season's, the Story's, climax.

Twice, Jesus weeps in the story. When He saw where death had laid out Lazarus, when He saw His friend's tomb, when He stood with the crying Mary, His Spirit moved over the face of the waters, and water ran down the face of God.

190

That's what Grandma had said: a man who can break down and cry is a man who will break open his heart to let your heart in.

Jesus wept. He had loved Lazarus. Our God is the God to find comfort in because ours is the God who cries . . . the God tender enough to break right open and let His heart run liquid, and He is the river of life because He knows our heart streams. One day He will wipe all tears away because He knows how the weeping feel: He has loved us.

I hold a crying Malakai and his bloody lip on a messy Palm Sunday and our tears and love mingle with God's.

Palm Sunday, the second time in the Story when the pain breaks Him and when the palm branches wave, our God weeps: when Jesus approached Jerusalem, "he wept over it and said, 'If you, even you, had only known on this day what would bring you peace . . .'"[56]

If only you had known what would bring you peace . . .

We want more comfort, and He offers us a cross. We want more position, and He offers us purpose. We want more ease, and He offers us eternity.

God cries because His people cry for things that won't bring them more peace. The people who praise Him on Palm Sunday on the way into the city are the same people who cry "crucify" loud on Good Friday when it doesn't go their way.

Don't believe things can change? Just look at Palm Sunday, to Good Friday, to Resurrection Sunday. Always believe, always keep hoping—things can change.

And yeah, I can be the woman who praises Him when it goes my way, and who complains loud when it doesn't. This is what happens when God doesn't meet expectations. When God doesn't conform to hopes, someone always goes looking for a hammer. I can bang my frustration loud.

The pastor would say it on Sunday—that the people's "Hosanna!" was a cry that literally meant "Save us! Save us!"

Jesus weeps because we don't know the peace that will save us. What brings us abundant peace is always abundant praise.

191

There are days when Christ comes to me in ways that look as lowly as coming on a donkey, and I'm the fool who doesn't recognize how God comes. God enters every moment the way He chooses and this is always the choice: wave a palm or a hammer.

How many times have I wondered how they could throw down their garments before Him on Sunday and then throw their fists at Him on Friday? But I'm the one in the front row: if our thanksgiving is fickle, then it turns out that our faith is fickle.

I stroke Malakai's forehead. Press mine to his.

"Can we just go get up and try again, Mama?" Malakai murmurs it, takes the cloth from his lip—and I see the wound. I wipe his wet cheek and hold him, just hold him long at the beginning of Holy Week, with these tears on the fingertips, ready for praise on the lips. Keeping company with the Christ who cries, His heart broken wide open to let us in.

And this Holy Week, there's a woman who wipes the drool from her father's chin and carries him down the hall to the toilet. And there's a mother who lays down bits of her singular life to wash the bowls and the underwear of the teenager calling her a whore. And there's a missionary far away from a microphone or a spotlight who bends in a jungle, in a brothel, in a slum, in a no-name, unseen part of the globe, and nobody applauds.

Are the realest sacrifices of praise *not* the ones shouted at the beginning of Holy Week, but the secret, sacred rites that are gifts of praise given back to Him, gifts to Him and the world, offered with no thought of return on investment, just given when the only spotlight is His light, and your one flaming heart?

Maybe Holy Week is the week you ask yourself: who's defining the terms when it's an honor to be awarded by people and a sacrifice to be called by God? Maybe the call of Holy Week isn't so much about trying to carry your cross across a lit stage, but about carrying your daily cross down the Via Dolorosa, taking the broken way of suffering. Maybe the

192

best way to let your life be a genuine hosanna to Him is to live given in places where it'd be easy for no hosannas to ever be sung.

The word *altar* has roots in the Latin *altus*, meaning "high." Because real altars are not where crowds see and applaud the sacrifice. But real altars and sacrifice are those that only He in the highest heaven sees.

And I nod to our boy at the beginning of Holy Week, "Yes, yes, let's try again." And the kid slides off my lap. And there's this walking together into Holy Week, daring to walk with this brazen, unwavering thanks to Him that bends low enough to serve in hidden ways.

The way to worship Christ is more than raising your hands like you're waving palm branches; it's stretching your arms out like you're formed like a cross.

Cruciform.

True worship isn't formed like a hand-waving crowd; true worship is formed living cruciform.

Holy Week begins with Palm Sunday, and the only way to live a holy life is with palms open wide. To live given and hidden and surrendered, cross-formed. *Abundantly cruciform.*

The silhouette of Christ there on the table, He carries a cross, leans forward like He's leaning into a cruciform story, leaning into abundant story that could be ours.

Who doesn't choke up and about weep that we could marry our vision to His, our hearts to His?

FOR REFLECTION

- ✧ How are you living in ways that are broken and given like bread— cruciform, in secret ways far away from the applause?
- ✧ Where can you bring a hosanna to Him, a sacrifice of praise, in thanksgiving for the abundant life He has given?

Devotion 48

PATIENT BROKENNESS

Be kind to one another, tender-hearted, forgiving each other,
just as God in Christ also has forgiven you.

EPHESIANS 4:32 NASB

I drive our limp rag doll girl into town to see the doctor. Five days straight of fever. I'm worried and worn a bit thin and why in the world does loving someone always make you feel so vulnerable?

Then: I lock the keys in the van. Mother of the Year Award right there. I use the doctor's phone to call our boys. "*Don't forget about us! We need* those keys to get home."

A long wait, a doctor visit, a prescription written, and an hour and forty-three minutes later . . . no dice. We're locked out of the doctor's office and the parking lot's empty. I'm stranded with an inferno child, only seven minutes from home. I want to break, curl up and bawl. Yes, it's teenagers and just a set of keys. But what kind of parent have I been? Whose kids completely forget about her in her crisis? I feel worse than abandoned—I feel like a failure. I haven't loved them enough to be loved back?

My logical self tries to curl comfort around the angst of all my drama: life is less about a formula and more about faith; life is more than Good In = Good Out, but more like when God's enough, there's grace enough. Life can't be about being good enough, but instead believing there is God

194

enough—God enough for whatever our own humanity needs grace for. And there's always that: today's bread is enough bread, today's grace is enough grace, today's God is enough God. The question is, can I believe that when the suffering and the grief and the anger and the frustration come? And if I can—will it make me feel any less alone?

I call home from a phone booth. When one of the boys finally shows up with the keys, I take them from him slowly. I know I'm overreacting and triggered, but there's some hot lava building to let loose in my veins, my heart liquefying, and there's no stopping it, things blurring and spilling a bit.

Turn the keys slow and easy because you've been here and done that and you know this: love means holding your tongue when your heart is hard. *Or when it's breaking.*

I wait, whisper it to myself, soothing, reassuring. "Love will always make you suffer. Love only asks, 'Who am I willing to suffer for?'" This is the severe grace of love making me real. Real love is patient and it bites its tongue. It lets its heart be broken like bread. I had never felt it quite so viscerally before: picking up your cross feels most like *patience.*

I'm standing there with keys in my hand. Love, before it is anything, to be love at all, it is first patient. And I'd experienced enough to know that patience is nothing but a willingness to suffer. Patience and the word *passion*, they both come from the exact same root word, *patior*, to suffer.

Passion has much less to do with elation and much more to do with patience. Passion embraces suffering because there's no other way to embrace love. Love isn't about feeling good about others; love is ultimately being willing to suffer for others.

Our boy standing there. How I do love him. And *oh, how do I love him?* Everything in me reverberates with that one thing I know again and again and again to be truest about love: *the moment you're most repelled by someone's heart is when you need to draw closer to that heart.*

So I say to him, "Sorry—sorry I haven't loved you like you've needed, son." Lay my hand slowly, fully on him, like a benediction. Like a gift.

And I can feel it—Christ within. No one gets to forgiveness unless something dies.

"No—*I'm* sorry, Mom."

I don't turn away from his eyes. Do you actually only love someone if, when they break your heart, you don't hate them?

And I nod at the boy, the relief of a slow smile breaking . . . and giving grace away . . . his way.

FOR REFLECTION

✧ Is there a place you are running from brokenness, either in your own life or someone else's? How can you pull closer to that broken heart, even when it hurts the most?

✧ How can you choose to suffer for someone today—to extend the gift of patience and forgive with abundant grace, as He has forgiven you?

Devotion 49

BLESS MY ENEMIES

"Do not judge, and you will not be judged. Do not condemn, and you will not be condemned. Forgive, and you will be forgiven."

LUKE 6:37

Not all enemies carry arrows.

All my life I liked to think it was only David who had his enemies. Is it easier to say we don't have any enemies, so we don't have to figure out how to really love them?

And how to forgive enemies from the heart? But who hasn't been cheated on, talked down, lied about, pierced right through, and left heart-broken on some beaten-down back road? There are a thousand ways to bleed, to nurse wounds and bitterness, and no one knows.

I have twisted limbs on my family tree, but no one burned the fig tree down. Just this one little girl burned with shameful memories, dirtiness right under her skin, and how to get clean? I remember asking my mama why some relatives are called grands.

How many years have I stood in sanctuaries and murmured that one line of the Apostles' Creed? "I believe in the forgiveness of sins." Have I really believed? Do all the creed keepers believe only in the forgiveness of their sins alone? Or do they, the Christ bearers, really believe in the forgiveness of sins and sinners?

Do we believe in a culture of wholesale forgiveness? Weren't we once the enemies? Aren't our enemies our kin? Don't we have to let them into grace?

My dad loved another woman and that other woman sometimes inadvertently hurt my mama while she slept in her bedroom and scrubbed Mama's memories out of her own house, and I've done my own spiteful share of burning. I'm the fig branch that often should have been hacked off.

I have bowed and said it aloud for decades. "Forgive us our debts, as we forgive our debtors." *Who really, actually, lives this?*

If we only got into the Christ-faith through the door of forgiveness, how can we claim Christ as our home if we aren't people who forgive? Words and ideology on a page are cheap. Grace and incarnating the love of Christ isn't.

I do want there to be another way—another way of abundance, where they pay their debt of pain. I forget that I haven't had to pay, me bought with the blood of God. If forgiveness isn't central to our faith, is our faith really Christian?

A stranger drove over my sister, and he drove home to his family. The grief of her gravestone drove us mad. My little brother and I used to imagine finding that man. Does "love your enemies" have any loopholes? How far can forgiveness go?

I have known this, though: an eye for an eye and a tooth for a tooth leaves us all starving and groping in the dark. In the evenings, in the dark setting in, I sit and knit a bit. There are lilacs on the table, a bouquet spraying over the vase, over the edge. A twisted old limb that somehow bore grace, somehow blossomed. And I move them, these two wooden needles, these two pieces of wood pointed, sharpened, at the ends.

I knit and pray my own wandering version of an old prayer for old pain:

Bless my enemies, O Lord. Even I bless them and do not curse them. Enemies have driven me into Your embrace more than friends have. Enemies have loosed me from earth more than friends have . . .

Enemies have made me a hunted animal, finding safer shelter than an unhunted animal does. I have found the safest sanctuary in You—may my enemies-made-grace also find it in You. I found greatest grace in You—may my enemies-made-grace find Your generous grace alive and radical in me. I found fullest forgiveness in You—may my enemies-made-grace find faith and freedom in You and Your forgiveness working surprising ways in me.

The longer I walk with You, Lord, I find I have no enemies—only Your gift of chisels etching me deep.

Bless my enemies, O Lord. Even I bless them and do not curse them.[57]

In the shadows, there is this—the murmured prayers and the needles with pointed edges touching each other, these needles looking like arrows, like they're looking for loopholes out of love. But then the needles do the unexpected—this slipping of delicate prayers around each other slow and an act of the will, this knitting and uniting.

These strings all knotting now close.

FOR REFLECTION

✧ In what one broken relationship in your life today can you trade any bitterness and resentment for the gift of forgiveness? What would that look like in practice?

✧ Visualize, feel it: How can you allow His abundant love to seep into your bones today, touch and cover even the deepest wounds and scars? What do you want to say to God right now?

Devotion 50

BREAKING DEEP

Count it all joy, my brothers, when you meet trials of various kinds.

JAMES 1:2 ESV

When I feel like we're drowning in it all a bit, our daughter Hope and I, we go up to the lake and feel the waves pound, feel the serene fury of water. Feel the waves breaking against the earth and it quakes the inner cochlea and there's nothing else to hear but the breaking.

Hope stands there with wind blowing strands of hair across her face, the electrical energy of each breath of wet, briny air sparking something in her.

"Is there anything lovelier, really, than the way waves keep touching the shore no matter what tries to keep pulling it away?" I lean into her, point down the foaming shoreline. Say it over the sound of the wind, of the crashing surf.

Hope tucks her hair behind her ear. "Love's like a wave—it keeps reaching out no matter what tries to keep pulling it away."

She and I stand there in the battering of the elements, watching waves, watching how the light catches in water, how the waves move like the earth's own pulse—*like our own heartbeat.*

"You know, a pool isn't like this." I say it slow, watching the waves, seeing it for the first time. "It has no power, no life, because it has no breaking of waves. *Strange how that is*: it's in the breaking that there's life."

Abundant life.

What did my husband say again and again? "Never be afraid of being a broken thing . . . Unless a seed breaks, there is no life."

All down the shoreline, right at our feet, the waves keep crashing and breaking . . . *and living.*

Hope slips her arm through mine. Her hair's blowing into mine. All life losses break us, break through us, scar us. I want them not to. Frankly, there are days I'd like to hide my scars and the jagged edges of my brokenness, days when I wish there were no marks to bear. *But if losses don't leave their mark, how can we say we were ever marked or shaped by love?* Scars can be signs that show the way we loved.

Sometimes . . . if your scars are deep, so was your love. And it's true. Scar tissue is stronger than original skin ever is. Scars are where the strength gets in—our breaking is where our strength gets in.

And scars are only ugly to people who can't see.

Hope's hand rests on mine. "Maybe I just gotta make my heart get tougher?" She turns toward me.

And I get it, I hear her heart, the way the girl beats. When tough things keep coming at you, you think you have to get tougher.

I say it quietly, not sure she hears me over the waves. "You know— hearts that get tougher leave you with nothing of value to give."

Love is what we have to give, and love comes from places that are vulnerable and soft and tender enough to feel—*to break.*

Only those who are vulnerable enough to be broken get to be the ones who really love. It can be that when you feel broken, it's proof that you've given. Is there anything greater than living heart-broken, wide open and given?

Hope pulls my hand high, and we both stand there with our hands flung up into the winds, beckoning the crashing waves. Who understands the language of waves? Life, fears, losses, grief, stresses—it all keeps coming like waves. You can feel like you're drowning, everything you need to hold on to, breaking up all around you.

And I don't even realize I'm saying it out loud. "When you're hit by the breaking waves, break deep."

You've got three options when the breaking waves of life, fears, grief, stresses, hit—when you feel like you're drowning. You can either *let fear make you fight hard*—but fear never makes you safe; fear just makes you fall and fall hard. Fear always makes you fall and no one can outrun a breaking wave. Or you can *fall back on your pride* and try to brace against that wave breaking over you—and it will break you.

Pride goes before the breaking.

When you're driven hard by the waves of life, it's tempting to be driven by either pride or fear. But this could happen—and there could be a breaking free of fears, breaking free of pride. When you're hit with a breaking wave, you can *break deep into that breaking wave* and let yourself be moved by Living Water and transformed and formed by Christ and remade by the rising current of His love.

The only way through the breaking waves is to break deep into the wave. Point your fingers in front of you and duck your head and plunge yourself into the wave. Forget fighting the waves, forget bracing against the waves—give yourself to the waves, enter into the waves, face and fingers first, breath held, and let them wash over you.

The only way through a wave breaking over you is to break deep into the roiling water and dive down into the depths and stretch out both arms through the fathoms and let yourself be made into the shape of a cross.

This is how you float, this is how you stay alive. Stretch out both arms, live formed like a cross. That's all there is: You can either be broken by fear or broken by pride, or you can break into the surrendered, cruciform shape of Christ. When you dive deep into the breaking waves and stretch out your arms like a cross, you find yourself in what they call the "cushion of the sea."

Far beneath the breaking waves, beneath the crashing storm of things, there is a space, a stillness of the sea that doesn't ever stir. That's never disturbed. Break into a shape of a cross, arms outstretched and surrendered—*and you break into the deep, deep peace of God.* In the midst of the storms, live shaped like a cross, arms broken wide open, and you can break into the still cushion of the sea.

Break deep. Break deep and roll.

I turn to Hope. There can be this feeling of being baptized. You can live through the breaking waves. You can break deep, break open wide and roll. What feels like surrender, this can feel like freedom.

When you're in over your head, you touch the depths of God. Break deep. *Break deep and roll.*

For Reflection

✧ When your breaking waves of life hit, what is your typical response? Do you respond with fear or pride—or do you choose to break deeper?

✧ Where is a place you need to break into a cross, outstretched and surrendered cruciform into the "cushion of the sea," the abundant grace of God?

Part Six

HOW DO THE
BROKENHEARTED
GET TO LOVE?

SOMETHING BEAUTIFUL

Jesus answered, "If you want to be perfect, go, sell your possessions and give to the poor, and you will have treasure in heaven. Then come, follow me."

MATTHEW 19:21

I wanna buy something."

That's what the woman tells me. You can see that look in her eyes, looking for something lovely. Something new and shiny and lovely that catches the light in its own way. Sometimes we want to possess lovely things because we don't know what love is.

"Something beautiful. I want something really beautiful."

Maybe, you know, *like a nicer house*? The kind of house to come home to, that looks like Joanna and Chip whipped it up, the kind that gets pinned as the pinnacle of Pinterest, that has soaring windows and climbing roses. Or a thatched roof and hobbit doors and a claw-foot tub. Or how about buying a silky new blouse? Slimming. Shimmering just a bit. Draping across the shoulders to make her look like an unexpected supernova that stops the unsuspecting dead in their slack-jawed tracks. *Just a bit.*

She could click through a dozen rabbit-hole sites, she could order a bit here, a bit there, and go ahead and fill a closet full of all the beautiful things, of lovely things: folded stacked quilts and old, wide windowsills full of clay pots of blooming geraniums reaching for spring sun, and fireplaces full of a choir of wavering, dripping candles, and white duvets turned back and always waiting.

When you know love is about self-giving, then maybe the loveliest things are not about self-having?

"Somedays I just want all the beautiful things. The Instagram white walls and the filtered warm light." She'd turned, caught light of her own. "Sometimes I wonder if we want a curated stream of beauty to make sense of our chaotic stream of consciousness?"

I nodded.

And then a woman turned to me in a car this week and asked me what I didn't see coming in the least. "So what do you want your life to really be about?"

We'd pulled up, she opened the car door, and I sat there fixed and yet a kind of jarred broken, staring out the windshield, heart unshielded. Exposed.

What do I really want? What do I want my one life to really be about? What you most want is what you most love. And what you love is what you'll ultimately have for all eternity.

And I'm thinking it's doubtful that you're thinking of pretty Instagram streams when you're standing at the river of life flowing like a torrent of glory from the throne room of God. Doubtful that you're still hankering for a house remodel when you're witnessing rag-tattered kids from the Kenyan slums running into the open arms of the King of Kings standing there at heaven's gates. Doubtful that you're standing at the feet of Jesus, thinking you wanted more threads in your closet when you could have been about more souls in the kingdom.

But there is no doubt that beautiful things can genuinely be made into meaningful things, beautiful can definitely be made into faithful things, and certainly, thank God Almighty, there is no definitive black-and-white line in the sand between beautiful and meaningful. But there are times when instead of trying forcefully to see the monied-beautiful as ministry-meaningful . . . we may be better off simply seeking out the most meaningful—and seeing *that* as the most beautiful.

The most fulfilling lives seek out the meaningful more than the beautiful. *Meaningful over beautiful.* The most fulfilling lives may actually see the *meaningful* as the most beautiful.

What, if any, craving for the beautiful is really a craving for Jesus? And Jesus may be found in impressive houses, but He's powerfully found with the kids pressed into rotting garbage piles, digging for a handful of food. He's found in everyone, in every need and every craving for help, in every face and every place we'll ever encounter.

Living the broken way of abundance isn't about what you love; it's about who you love.

And Jesus is always who we love.

Let all the houses of cards come crashing down so there can be resurrection to greater things.

A tragic life is a life driven by social media likes instead of Christ-motivated loves. Because honestly it would be a travesty to have a life about collecting pretty things instead of recollecting that we were made for greater things.

You're meant for more than collecting seashells.

When I light the candles on the Lenten wreath, the flames waver.

Let this Lent dismantle everything that isn't about eternal things.

You were meant for greatness, and greatness is about serving greatly.

The Lenten candles on the wreath are disappearing, melting lower, giving themselves into light. God doesn't call you to a convenient life; He calls you to an important life. *And a life of importance isn't found in a life of convenience.*

A life of importance sees the import of giving your life away, to the hidden and the unpopular and the children and the forgotten and knowing this will be remembered by God.

Flames flicker brave, flicker on against the dark. The most beautiful lives live for the most meaningful.

You weren't meant for self-gratification; you were meant for *soul* greatness. Never settle for immediate gratification, because you are called to eternal greatness.

I met a woman once who said she wanted to buy what was beautiful. But then her soul turned around and decided to pay attention to all the broken and beautiful ways to live what is meaningful. Her people said she had no idea how she became, over time, more and more like light.

Like all the meaningfulness of abundant light.

FOR REFLECTION

- ✧ Where do you find yourself living for self-gratification, choosing beautiful things over the seeming chaos of broken and beautiful people?
- ✧ What are some ways you can find the most abundant life, and choose the meaningful over the beautiful? How is God calling you right now?

Devotion 52

PRESSING THINGS

Praise be to the God and Father of our Lord Jesus Christ,
the Father of compassion and the God of all comfort.

2 CORINTHIANS 1:3

P ress on," is what the guy said as he nodded my way and walked out the door of the church.

Press on . . .

The sky scuttled low and grey after church, close to the steeples, catching on the silos dotting farms and our back roads, like the bellied underside of heaven pushing up against earth. I didn't just hear his words echoing all the way home; I could feel them, pressing a bit like a vise. Coming from all sides, all this pressure in a fallen world that just keeps falling upon us. You can feel it. The pressing of time, of brokenness, of bills, of work and deadlines and expectations, of life. A day, a season, a life, can press you down to flattened discouragement.

Discouragement is a hijacker. It presses you up against a wall, empties your pockets of purpose, steals your joy, chokes your hope. It creeps up on you, unexpected, and suddenly you are robbed of hope, of joy, of *abundance.*

But other words murmur after church all the way home: "Blessed be the God and Father of our Lord Jesus Christ, the Father of mercies and God of all comfort, who comforts us in all our affliction."[58] You have more than a friend in your affliction; you have a Father, a Father of "mercy"—*oiktirmos* in the Greek. It means compassion—co-suffering—pity, mercy, and not merely a considered thought, but a feeling from the heart.

When your heart feels pressed up against a wall, the heart of your very own Father feels mercy. He co-suffers with you and knows what your "affliction" feels like—*thlipsis* in the Greek literally translates "a pressing, a pressure." And in the midst of the pressure from all sides, the phrase He "comforts us," *paraklesis*, is far more than even an empathetic sentiment; it literally means God's comfort is being "called to one's side to strengthen."

When you are stressed, you have a God who strengthens. When you are flattened, you have a God who fortifies. When you are crushed, you have a God who comforts. When you are broken, you have a God who breaks you free from hopelessness.

The Holy Spirit is our comforter and the Holy Spirit is our strengthener—One who supernaturally sympathizes and strengthens the brokenhearted supernaturally. When you think you don't have any strength left, you have a Strengthener who never leaves you.

There's a wind coming in from the west, bending the saplings in the ditches along the last gravel road home from church. It comes too, like the Spirit's wind, like a mercy, what affects the way and bend of everything today: when more suffering comes, more of God's strength comes.

When strengthened by the Holy Spirit through our pressures, we get to express the Holy Spirit life to others under pressure. Our brokenness can offer others a comfort that is more than sympathy. Our brokenness can offer a comfort that literally strengthens.

This is the way of conversion, the way He makes brokenness into abundance. Christ was crushed and through this He comforts us; Christ suffers and through His suffering He strengthens us—*saves* us.

And now we share, participate in, have communion, *koinonia*, in the sufferings of Christ—and through our co-suffering with Christ, who suffers with us in our afflictions and pressures, we comfort and strengthen and break others free into more of Christ.

The very first word of the body of Paul's second letter to the Corinthians is blessing and praise to God—right in the midst of burdens and pressures and brokenness. Every real conversion to Christ means exercising the faith we're given and relentlessly converting problems to praise.

Because there are blessings in burdens, there is grace in the grind, and there is abundance being made out of even this brokenness.

That night after church, I walk the floor for hours, our baby crying loud and long into the night, and I can feel decades of givenness pressing. I can feel all the things I can't control pressing. *In the midst of my pressing—Christ's abundant strength presses into me. Christ is with me. Immanuel, God with me. His with-ness breaks my brokenness.*

Kind of bleary with weariness, I stroke back the wailing baby's hair, try to smooth her forehead.

I could feel it then—what was happening in the pressing.

And I knew—I could re-member—what all this pressing meant.

The only way anything can ever become a fragrance—is for something to surrender itself to being crushed and broken open.

Every perfume, every cologne, every fragrance, always involves a crushing, a pressing, a breaking. The only way to be the abundant fragrance of Christ—is to let your life be pressed and broken open by Christ. The only way to become the fragrance of Christ—is to take the broken way of abundance.

Under an inky, starry sky, I curl a crying baby in close and try to surrender to whatever comes—*givenness . . . givenness*. Never be afraid of broken things, never be afraid of pressing things—He is making them into fragrant things. He is using the pressing things—to break us open into the scent of God.

And our baby howls louder and I lean in, kiss her hair, her forehead, hold the scent of her closest. Wanting to fix broken things, change broken places, make broken hearts whole, it isn't being the fragrance of Christ—but trying to usurp Christ Himself. We aren't called to fix broken people—we are called to be *with* broken people. It is *Christ* who makes abundance out of brokenness. Even in all her wailing, she smells like a bit of heaven next to me. Even the darkest night can carry the scent of light.

And there is an epiphany in the dark: presence is the essence of being the fragrance of Christ. *Koinonia*—communion—is the call of Christ. Our being pressed into the fragrance of Christ begs us to simply press close to other broken and pressed hearts—so they may be strengthened by the scent of Christ. The pressures of life mean to make us into the fragrance of Christ. And with-ness is the fragrance of Christ. And ultimately—with-ness breaks brokenness.

When she finally falls asleep, her cheek is pressed against mine. And pressing, any afflictions, can be a breaking open—into the abundant fragrance of Christ.

The wind picks up, a gust through the spruce trees, and there is a pressing on.

---------------------- FOR REFLECTION ----------------------

- ✧ What brokenness is pressing in on you today in ways you feel you can't escape?
- ✧ How can you press this brokenness you've identified into Christ, and allow Him to break you open into the abundant scent of Christ, into the most abundant life? How can you press yourself close to other broken and pressed hearts, trusting that with-ness truly breaks brokenness?

Devotion 53

THE EMMAUS OPTION

"Were not our hearts burning within us?"

LUKE 24:32

Mountain rock is fleetingly temporary compared to the forever permanence of the rock of His Word.

The trail here at Lost Valley Ranch winds up these mountains ragged and torn with the thorns of a million fired trees. The horses climb higher, like they're finding a way through. They say it will take 150 years to heal and return these mountainsides. Who knows how long for a land scorched by injustice and singed with ache to quietly humble and pray and heal and return?

This is true—you can feel it in the wind: when it feels like your world's burning down, there are no really good formulas. There is simply being real, and keeping your eyes on Him who is always good.

The spacious sky up here is begging us to look up. To be still and know . . . Jesus doesn't need us to be His militants in a broken world as much as He invites all of us who've been mangled by this broken world to simply point to our Mender. And who knows why it comes right then, no idea at all why it comes right then, but the prophet Amos echoes across these burned and tree-barren hillsides: "'The days are coming,' declares the Sovereign LORD, 'when I will send a famine through the land—not a famine of food or a thirst for water, but a famine of hearing the words of the LORD. People will stagger from sea to sea and wander from north to east, searching for the word of the LORD, but they will not find it.'"[59]

In a broken world that may not esteem the Bible but still esteems Jesus, it's Jesus who says that Scripture cannot be broken. So what is our way through a post-Christian culture? What are our options to love the wounded, bind up the hurting, dress all the bleeding with grace and truth, and edify the body from the inside so that we can live out the Great Commission to the outside?

When our neighbors are different from us and think different than we do, when faith communities and colleagues hold different opinions and vision than ours, what is our option? There's been talk of a "Benedict Option," this idea of pioneering forms of retreating from a post-Christian culture to create intentional faith communities, "an intentional and thoughtful retreat into [the narrative] . . . [to live] the church's story, inculcating commitment to it within the lives of its members."[60] It's an idea with merit, an idea with history.

But here I am on a scarred mountainside in the middle of a summer that's burning up the edges of everything, wondering what would happen if the people of the cross took the Emmaus road through this landscape, the "Emmaus Way," and lived out the "Emmaus Option."

As they talked and discussed these things with each other, Jesus himself came up and walked along with them; but they were kept from recognizing him . . . And beginning with Moses and all the Prophets, he explained to them what was said in all the Scriptures concerning himself . . .

When he was at the table with them, he took bread, gave thanks, broke it and began to give it to them. Then their eyes were opened and they recognized him . . . They asked each other, "Were not our hearts burning within us while he talked with us on the road and opened the Scriptures to us?"[61]

Jesus walks with us here, but how do we recognize Him or truth or the grace of cross-shaped love that can make sense of what is happening in culture right now?

What if there were a way of radical grace and truth through a post-Christian landscape? Such an option might begin by suggesting the breaking open of Scriptures to see how every page is scarred with the passion of Christ. It could involve the breaking of our plans and agendas to stay by people, stay close to people, stay with people. And it could lead us to prioritize the breaking of bread with people, the breaking of cynicism to give thanks, the daily gift of being broken and given to the people around us.

Isn't this the broken way of abundance? Could such an "Emmaus Option" open eyes, open minds, tenderly open broken and busted hearts, and kindle them with life, as Jesus did, using every gift God's given to make the world greater? Our way through any broken landscape may always be this simple. The body of Christ must recapture its vision as the only collective in the world that exists for its *nonmembers*. We are a community that exists for the exiled, the reviled, the profiled, and the longing-to-be-reconciled.

We're a community that lives our calling to such offensive grace that it looks like we're soft on truth, routinely accused of being gluttons and drunkards because the King of our kingdom lived around addicts, prostitutes, and shady tax collectors, the broken-down, the busted-up, and the religiously disdained. And He never once explained Himself, only continually gave of Himself.

If Jesus welcomed sinners and ate with them, why would we position ourselves to sit at any other table?

We're a community that will not dish out condemnation but courage, that will lean in and listen long and love large. We define success as showing up and bending down, serving well over debating well, serving after the lights go off because there's a light in *us*.

Be the bread broken and given to a hungry world that *yearns* for the taste of such glory.

And this could make all our broken hearts burn within us again.

The light caught in the mountains, and it's strange how it makes the valley look like the hollow of cupped hands, the edges blazing with an epiphany of hope. You can be standing there and feel the burning of your broken heart within, kindling.

FOR REFLECTION

- ✧ In what ways do you need to break your own selfishness, to truly live broken and given, choosing to let go of your plans and agendas and give wholeheartedly to the hearts of others?
- ✧ Where can you live the "Emmaus Option" in your own community, breaking your agenda, breaking open Scripture, breaking bread with outsiders, breaking cynicism to give thanks—to break free into the abundant life? How is God pointing to the Emmaus Option in your life today?

Devotion 54

UNDENIABLE EVIL

"If you are returning to the LORD with all your hearts, then rid yourselves of the foreign gods . . . and commit yourselves to the LORD and serve him only, and he will deliver you."

1 SAMUEL 7:3

There's a dusting of snow in the orchard. The trees are white and perfectly still out in the woods. There's dust on the windowsills by the stove. Wiping down the sills and the countertops and the stove, it's like a refrain in my head:

We're all just dust. Just dust.

And if I'm only dust, just my love alone in the world will not be enough. If love is all we need in this world—I've got a problem.

Because if I'm honest, my love isn't enough to absorb the evil, the supernatural evil that slithers into the corners of this world and pythons around hearts and minds until it strangles out the light and we scream against the dark.

At some point—in a broken world, your love runs out, and you need a love larger than your own to love larger than evil. The only love that can take down the kind of evil that's invaded our world has to come from beyond the walls of the world. The only love that can crush undeniable evil is the undeniable love of the cross. When you're just dust, your love alone will not be enough.

Super evil can only be absorbed by a supernatural kind of love.

The kind of love that sings "kumbaya" can't shake a swaying candle at this kind of otherworldly evil. Only an otherworldly love that lets the hammer ring and took on the iron of the nails, that bore the weight of the world on that cross, can torch straight through the hellish dark of this kind of evil.

Sometimes, for the love, your heart can't love—which is exactly why Jesus offers you His. For God so loved the world that He gave . . . The whole story isn't "everyone's in." It's "everybody's invited." Everybody's wanted. Everybody's loved. Everybody's given the invitation. Absolutely every single person is invited in.

Our love will eventually fail and leave somebody out—but cross love never fails to take all the willing in. His love has no boundaries—and then He binds all the beloved to Him, to shape them to be like Him. And He knows the only way for your love to be transformed to be like His—is for Him to give you a heart transplant. For Him to give you His heart.

When you don't think you can forget the evil that's been done, said—when it's His supernatural heart beating in you—it lets you supernaturally love in a heartbeat. Only the undeniable love of the cross can crush undeniable evil.

If there's evil—not merely people acting, but real, active evil—out to terrorize the world, attack young girls, take advantage of the vulnerable, blow us up, and behead us—then kumbaya love will never be enough; only cross love that willingly offers itself for us as a living ransom will rescue any of us.

It comes back to me a thousand times, how a missionary told of this snake—a snake longer than a man—that had wound its way up the stilts of a jungle cabana and slithered right into one unsuspecting woman's kitchen.

And that woman had turned around, split the day with one bloodcurdling scream, and flung herself outside wide-eyed. That's about when a machete-wielding neighbor had showed up, calmly walked into her kitchen, and sliced off the head of the reptilian thing.

But the strange thing is that a snake's neurology and blood flow make it such that a snake still slithers wild even after it's been sliced headless.

For hours that woman stood outside, waiting.

And the body of the snake still rampaged on, thrashing hard against windows and walls, destroying chairs and table and all things good and home.

A snake may wreak havoc—but it has no head. It's actually dead.

Even if the tail still rampages, the snake's head is crushed.

There may be the thrashings of evil—but it is ultimately crushed.

Only the undeniable love of the cross can crush undeniable evil.

Either Jesus is the answer to the ultimate problems of the human condition—or there is no ultimate answer.

Because don't ever be fooled: cross love that lays itself down is the only power that can lay the sharp edge of an axe right into evil's head. Cross love that looks weak, surrendered, and sacrificed is the only strong power that ultimately upends the evil and conquers the dark.

Maybe now is the time to bend our knees and let ourselves be counted as the people of the cross. Maybe that's all there is for today: For we the people of the cross to repent of wanting to be greatly known for anything other than for loving greatly. To repent of a love and life that does anything less than "love your enemies and pray for those who persecute you."[62] And to repent of not daily, relentlessly, extravagantly loving our neighbor next door though we keep saying we want to change the world. Can we repent of hating, avoiding, and dreading suffering though we say we want to be found worthy to suffer for the cross of Christ? Can we repent of loving our agendas more—instead of interrupting our agendas because we love Jesus most?

We repent of loving You, Lord, so little because we have loved ourselves too much.

So, what if we looked to the cross—so we might become cruciform, cross love in a world caught in the crosshairs of war and heartache and pain? What if we looked to the cross and prayed 1 Samuel 7:3 at 7:03? "Return to the Lord with all your heart . . ." And what if we said our amens with 2 Chronicles 7:14: "If my people, who are called by my name, will humble themselves and pray and seek my face and turn from their wicked ways, then I will hear from heaven, and I will forgive their sin and will heal their land."

Could this help us become cruciform and turn back to our first love, take back our hypocrisy and our complacency and our apathy to love lavishly, take back our excuses for not committing to give back every day in some tangible, real way?

Maybe now is the time to take back what it means to humbly and genuinely live the love of the people of the cross.

One spring here on the farm, long after the snow had melted out in the orchard and the cold had gone and the strange white wilderness had resurrected into green, I lay in a bare field west of the barn, stretched out on warm, turned-over farmland. And I held dust, right there in my hand. Dust holding dust. And I could feel that dust and know that it was a good soil for breaking open the otherworldly miracle of seeds pouring from the Farmer's hand. That revival would rise right up from the dust, spread like love across the land.

—————— FOR REFLECTION ——————

- ✧ In what ways are you relying on your own broken heart, your own limited love, your own finite self, instead of loving with His supernatural, cruciform cross love?
- ✧ Where do you need to turn back to His abundant life, to repent and pick up your cross and become cruciform, living broken and given, trading apathy for abundantly supernatural love? How is God calling you to repent, pray, and become more cruciform?

Devotion 55

AN INCONVENIENT LIFE

"For whoever wants to save their life will lose it, but whoever loses their life for me will save it."

LUKE 9:24

How do you know how to hold space for all this brokenness and not be afraid? This cross on my wrist—it's been showing me how to hold pain, to hold the pain of little deaths. To not be afraid of it, to not fight it. The cross allows you to hold pain—because that cross is absorbing all your pain.

Loving by halves is not how anyone becomes whole.

It leaks through the beating of our broken hearts: there are many ways, but there's only one way that leads to life. The performing way of the world is about impressing people, about creating your own parade of accomplishments. And the cruciform way of Christ is about letting the love of God and the needs of people impress and form you into a cross, being the Samaritan who sacrifices to help the other wounded paraders.

One way leads to a dead end, the other to love. What drives us to try to build a successful life rather than a meaningful life?

My friend Elizabeth, before she died of cancer, poured out her bucket—and by doing so, she let us all in on her secret: that a willingness to be inconvenienced is the ultimate proof of love. This is what dying to live means: You love as much as you are willing to be inconvenienced. Why hadn't I ever seen this before? The best investment of your life is to love exactly when it's most inconvenient. If I won't be inconvenienced, I can't know love. Am I willing to live an inconvenient life? The brokenness of people is never truly an intrusion. Loving broken people when it is inconvenient is the way to have fuller inclusion in the life of Christ.

Teach me to number my days, O Lord, that I may gain a heart of wisdom.[63]

The real sinew of community, the muscle of *koinonia*, is not in how well we impress each other but in how well we inconvenience ourselves for each other.

"I am certain that I never did grow in grace one half so much anywhere as I have upon the bed of pain," assured Spurgeon.[64] "I am not a theologian or a scholar," Elisabeth Elliot said, "but I am very aware of the fact that pain is necessary to all of us. In my own life, I think I can honestly say that out of the deepest pain has come the strongest conviction of the presence of God and the love of God."[65]

The most crushing lie a life can hold on to is that we are supposed to avoid suffering, avoid loss, avoid anything that breaks. Loss is our very air; we, like the certain spring rains, are always falling toward the waiting earth, but we can forget this. We desperately try to forget this. My friend Elizabeth, she remembered, and she showed us how to be broken and given into His waiting arms. Her life was spent in inconvenience, loving so beyond limits that it broke our hearts.

Loving people without expecting anything in return always turns out to have the greatest returns.

✧ How are you holding space for all the brokenness of life and living not afraid? How has living outstretched in cruciform givenness been showing you how to hold space for brokenness, to not be afraid of it, to not fight it, because the cross is absorbing all your pain?

✧ Why are you afraid of being inconvenienced? Where is God calling you to be more inconvenienced to experience abundant community and connection?

Devotion 56

GRATEFUL ABUNDANCE

The steadfast love of the LORD *never ceases;*
his mercies never come to an end;
they are new every morning;
great is your faithfulness.

LAMENTATIONS 3:22–23 ESV

I sat across from a woman who just kept looking up at the ceiling to keep herself from falling apart. Looked at the ceiling like she was looking for answers from somewhere on high. Looked at the ceiling and told me she loved God and she hated God and right now was the best of times and the worst of times and that's when she dropped her eyes hard like a gavel and half-demanded an answer: "And why does God strangely bless us when we're half-estranged from Him?"

It came out of her in one breath, like the exhale of a life. I waited and looked into her, not quite knowing how to breathe.

Sometimes the proof that God exists is that lightning doesn't strike, but quiet grace rains straight down. Sometimes it's incomprehensible grace that shakes you awake.

And when she bent her head low, chin to chest, and she broke open like a rain and there was no hiding it, I went around to her and I held her. I held her.

Because six years can be an exhausting eternity when you're in that ring dodging the horns of job loss and long hours and looming bills and accounts disappearing. When you need a new septic system, a new alternator, a new dream—and a really possible dream this time because the old one's been busted and Krazy Glued one too many shattered times. When everybody else has found their niche and their address and their way and you're wondering if Someone has lost your number because you keep waiting and yours never gets called and why does it feel like everyone else is moving ahead and everything in your world is falling behind and apart?

I hold her and sometimes it is best to re-break so you can heal right. Arm around her, around the shoulder-racked sobs, I can feel her finally feeling, feel all the weariness letting go, all the wounds bleeding clean, and this is where healing begins.

Why is it always much easier to forget that He *likes* us? We need to keep looking for the gifts, all the ways He loves.

It's true, it did sometimes feel juvenile and pointless, but the kingdom of heaven belongs to those who come like a child, and the counting of a thousand gifts had added up to joy. Why would anyone decide they don't want joy? But I suppose Naaman didn't want to wash seven times in the river either.[66]

Sometimes the great thing that heals us is doing a small thing again and again.

It isn't a week after I held her that I hold a feverish son racked with pneumonia. He called to me in the dark, in the still of the lateness and the lights all out. "Mama? *Mom?*"

And I came thinking fever and he coughed hard, and then he said it raspy, "They sang this line at Sunday evening church, and I knew when I heard it I had to tell you."

He called me to come for this?

And he coughs like he's breaking open, breaking like a storm, right into the crook of his bent arm: "If grace is an ocean, we're all sinking."

And he rolls over into his pillow. Rolls into sleep holding his chest

227

hurting hard. He's sick. He says it hurts to breathe. But he's called me in the middle of the night because if grace is an ocean, we're all sinking.

Why does God bless us when we're half-estranged from Him?

And I lay my hand on our boy's back. He doesn't know that I know that song—maybe because I don't always live like I know it. And it's for the cough-racked boy and the sob-racked sister and a time-racked world swathed in this amnesia: God's mercies are new every morning—not as an obligation to you, but as an affirmation of you.

It's right there in the sky every morning: every sunrise proves the burn of His passionate heart.

The car can fail today and the kids and the dog and the fire detector and the dishwasher and the doctor and the whole world and its entire economic system, but the mercies of God cannot and will not fail and His faithfulness is not merely great; it is unwavering.

The God who so loved this cracked world that He gave, He hasn't ever stopped giving. He won't stop. It's His very mercy that gets us from one moment to the next, and we're all walking around in an atmosphere of brazen affection.

Why does He still bless us? Any grace at all is always the most amazing of all.

I rub our son's back. And that's the answer I'll tell him in the new mercies of the morning, the answer I will tell the woman asking why it's so hard to live loved: that the word in Romanian for thank you is *mulțumesc* [multsu'mesk], a contraction of the Latin phrase *multum est*, "it is much." It is more than enough; it is much. It is abundant. A woman from Romania, she'd told me, "How much of my life has been crippled by anxiety, guilt, self-condemnation, and all the ugly rest! All because I hadn't known I was so utterly cherished by God."

Why is it so much easier to forget that He loves us? That He likes us?

His love is so much. It is *abundant*. When I feel like I'm sinking, there's a way to know that I'm sinking in an ocean of grace.

Nothing is too much to handle when I think about the so-much from His hand. The way out of the *pressing* too-much, is to whisper "thank you" for the *providential* so-much.

The boy breathes hard. This world is hard as nails and Christ knew it. That's why He came. He strangely blesses the half-estranged because the half-estranged are His beloved. It is much—abundant. That is the answer for every question in every language.

The kid inhales and I think it's so-much and so real for all the breaking ones: we breathe His abundant love—the healing comes with each breath we take in this ocean of grace.

FOR REFLECTION

✦ What are the broken places in your life that cause you to struggle to feel loved and accepted, to question if you are enough? Let God touch you in those places today with His abundant much-ness.

✦ Where is God asking you to thank Him for His abundant much-ness? How can you live in grateful awareness of the mystery of abundance you are living in today?

ESTHER GIVENNESS

"Give, and it will be given to you. A good measure, pressed down, shaken together and running over, will be poured into your lap. For with the measure you use, it will be measured to you."

LUKE 6:38

I'd read it once, how one in four people in a small town was deaf. And every one of them felt like an outsider. Until everyone in town learned sign language. The non-deaf disadvantaged themselves, inconvenienced themselves, to learn sign language. And it was the non-deaf whose lives were enhanced in unexpected ways. Not only did they gain rich relationships with deaf neighbors they would have missed out on otherwise, but they also discovered the convenience of signing across the street to one another, of sign language communicating from atop hills to folks below, of the sick signing what they needed when voices failed, of children signing to avoid being loud. Disadvantaging themselves turned out to be their advantage. *Brokenness was made into abundance.*

"To 'do justice,'" writes Tim Keller, "means to go to places where the fabric of shalom has broken down, where the weaker members of societies are falling through the fabric, and to repair it."[67]

We are each singular threads in the world. We all get to decide what we will tie our lives to. If I tie my resources, my time, only to the thin thread of my own life—my life's a hopelessly knotted mess.

The thread of your life becomes a tapestry of abundant colors only if it ties itself to other lives. The only way to strengthen the fabric of society is to let threads of your life break away to let Christ, who is in us, weave around other threads. "Reweaving shalom means to sacrificially thread, lace, and press our time, power, goods, and resources into the lives and needs of others . . . The strong must disadvantage themselves for the weak, the majority for the minority, or the community frays and the fabric breaks."[68]

The only way to care for the disadvantaged is to disadvantage yourself, *which is guaranteed to turn out to your advantage.*

We all could have been the disadvantaged outside the gate. We all could have been someone fallen on hard times into hard ways; we could have been the one fighting marauders threatening to slit our children's throats in the middle of the night; we could be the ones born into a slum, violently raped, and left for dead; the ones born into AIDS, into starvation, into lives of Christ-less desperation. The reason you are an Esther, inside the gate for such a time as this, is to risk your life for those outside the gate.

If I perish, I perish.

There are so many of us sucking down lattes and dying of thirst, dying for something more, for something abundant. There are so many in need, and so many Esthers who thirst for more than vanilla services, sweetened programs, and watered-down lives, hungry for some real meat for their starved souls, some dirt under the fingernails, some real sacrifice in the veins. I know why I keep writing a cross on my wrist.

There are those who are saved, but only by the skin of their teeth because they cared most about the comfort of their own skin and only minimally about anyone else's. They will have a hardly abundant entrance awaiting them in heaven. But those will not be the Esthers. There are those

231

who would rather turn a blind eye to the needy than turn to the needy and be like Christ. Those who would love playing at being Christian more than actually being one and loving giving. But those will not be the Esthers.

There's a whole generation of Esthers who want to be the gift, want to give it forward, whatever's in our hands, who want holy more than hollow. There's a whole Esther generation, and it is we who want the abundant life of going lower to love the least, the lonely, and the lost. The world needs people who will defy cynical indifference by making a critical difference.

Every one of us can start changing headlines when we start reaching out our hands.

We can be concerned for the poor—but be no less concerned for us rich who claim not to be rich so we can excuse ourselves from giving. Go ahead and show concern for the poor, but be no less concerned if we've merely done enough to assuage our consciences, just enough to pat ourselves on the back, but not enough that we've ever felt true sacrifice, that we've ever actually *broken* and given.

What if caring for the poor was more than just caring about easing our consciences? What if caring for the poor means sacrifice, and what if this is the way to be *satisfied* and know abundant living?

It isn't *having* that makes us rich; it's *giving*. Give sacrificially, live richly. Maybe all we really want is more of God. Abundance of Him.

FOR REFLECTION

- ✧ Where in your life do you see your soul too tightly tied to comfort, to advantages, or to things, so tightly tied that it's causing a kind of soul brokenness?
- ✧ How do you sense God calling you to be an Esther for such a time as now, to sacrifice and disadvantage yourself to risk like Esther, to live broken and given so you can know abundant living?

PASSING THE PEACE

"A new command I give you: Love one another. As I have loved you, so you must love one another."

JOHN 13:34

We're all more beautiful than we know because we're known and seen and loved in ways we don't know.

Not one of us ever walks alone.

In New York, the loveliest lady leaned over to me at the check-in counter and said, "I think I know you, and we're already friends!" This is always a true story no matter where we are. There is no such thing as a stranger; we are all already friends just waiting to meet.

The world may be hurting, but the world is holy.

And I shook her hand like an awkward fool, grabbed a pen, and gifted her a bunch of book pages with my broken heart scrawled all across it, and she reached for my hand. "Our girl was airlifted to a city hospital last night because she needs an organ transplant and our whole world . . . and she . . . and . . . we're just . . . *heartbroken.*"

And I pulled her in close and we held on and sometimes falling apart together is how things fall together.

There is no such thing as other people's children. All children are all of our children. When one of us grieves, we all grieve, and when one of us feels pain, we all feel pain, and there is no such thing as us and them, but us *with* them, which means there is just all of us.

Then her husband gathered round us and choked it back, his hand resting on her shoulder. "Remember the word He's given us: Fear not. Believe."

He turns to me. "I carry these verses around in my pocket. Hand them out to people. A Word for the day. *A gift.* And that's one God gave for us, back when our daughter first got so sick: *Fear not. Believe.*"

Those are the words that the Maker of the world has given the entire world: Fear not a grim forecast. Believe in the casting of a vision for more grace, more goodness, more God—an abundance of God. Fear not all the unknown things. Believe the God who knows all things. Fear not each other. Believe in the best of each other.

Fear not. Hope always. And hope has hands and hope leans into where it hurts and hope gets to work so that hoped-for things can rise.

We stand there in the middle of the airport and we all hold hands, one mama flying to her hospitalized daughter and one believing father who hands out the gift of God's Word to people he passes throughout the day. And we pray because this is where hope always begins, and hope never ends when prayers never end.

People, meet people. Humans, meet humans. Because this is who we are meant to be. We find each other, we ache with each other, we hear each other, we hold on to each other, and we pray for each other.

It's true that it happens on Sundays, just before they pass the bread and the wine, but it's happening too on street corners, happening in store aisles, happening in airports and offices and checkout lines, the way we, the people, pass the peace. You may not hear the quiet murmurings of *"the peace of Christ to you,"* like you do on Sunday mornings, but you can witness it everywhere. The way an elderly man passes the peace of a smile to the woman picking over tomatoes in the vegetable department, the way one dad with kids passes the peace of a nod to another dad juggling a screaming toddler and uncooperating stroller, the way we pass the peace and hold a door open for each other, the way we hold space for each other to think differently, live differently, see differently, the way we respect and love no matter what is different between us.

If we passed the peace to every person we pass throughout the day, maybe some of the broken, painful things would pass? Maybe when we pass the peace to each other, we can find a peace that passes all understanding.

This whole universe is Grace University. And honoring one another is how you get an honorary degree at Grace University. Everywhere, we get to learn. Everywhere is a class. Everything begins with the next face you see, the next person you stand beside. There is no greater grant you can receive—than to grant grace.

Now is when we don't grow cold to love. Now is when we can't let our need to be heard make us deaf to where we need to love. We can't let our increasing need to be heard decrease our need to be compassionate. Because if our hearts no longer have compassion, then our hands no longer have anything to offer the world.

Compassion literally means co-suffering. And it's only when we are willing to co-suffer with people that we get to say we have compassion for people. And it's only when we have compassion for people that we get to become more like Christ.

And one lovely woman in the Buffalo airport asks me to keep praying for her girl and I keep nodding yes. Who of us isn't in need of an organ transplant? Who of us doesn't need a new heart?

She lets me pray with her and she shares how she walks the broken way of humility and vulnerability and generosity, giving me bits of her broken heart. And she lets me carry a bit of her brokenness and invites me to have compassion, to co-suffer a bit with her. And this is a kind of healing. I try to memorize the beauty of her.

It's never the things you carry that hurt you, but how you carry those things. There is a beautiful broken way that offers a new way. There is a beautiful way we can all be together.

There is autumn in the wind, there are geese flying south over corn-fields. There are roads and ways to be taken and people meeting people, people fearing not and hoping always, and abundant peace being passed between us all, like gifts falling as quiet as a mid-November rain.

FOR REFLECTION

- ✧ In what ways is brokenness holding you in fear today, preventing you from living in His abundant, perfect peace? How can you live givenness and pass the peace today?
- ✧ When we live compassionately, we invite each other into our suffering, and we offer up bits of our broken, hurting hearts to each other. Where are some areas where you can co-suffer with another, and invite co-sufferers in, to pass peace to each other and experience abundant healing together?

Devotion 59

ABUNDANT LOVE

For God so loved the world that he gave . . .

JOHN 3:16

L et your heart live unguarded—and you let love capture you.

I wrote that one down on a piece of paper.

Folded it up and stuck it in my back pocket, like I'd been given the answers to the only test I ever needed to pass.

Live with an unguarded heart—and you let love capture you.

In the upside-down kingdom, you have to guard your heart from being wrongly guarded.

A few weeks ago, I turned to a friend after dinner, when we were walking back down the street, straight into the wind, and I straight up told her that I needed a shield or two to protect my heart.

"Put your heart out on a table—and it might get mistaken for dinner. It might get cut up and eaten alive." I didn't tell her how my own heart burned from razor-sharp words. Didn't tell her who had said what, didn't tell her how I had looked in a mirror, brushed back whatever was leaking and spilling and had vowed—Don't put your heart down on the table again, or it will get knifed.

I knew it with my head:

Transparency is the glass door that opens up a house of trust so love can get in. But my tender and busted heart? The head can know wisdom, but the heart knows its wounds.

When my mama stood in the kitchen the other day, over a pot at the stove, I watched how she stirred with a hand missing part of a finger. There are women who walk around with parts of themselves wounded and missing. But they have found their soul, their way—they have found the good life.

Mama serves me her soup. She looks me in the eye and my mama reads my pain, all the liquid heartbreak I keep blinking back. "You know—living 'light and polite' is not really living. Living 'light and polite' can be a way of keeping everyone in the dark about what's in your heart."

Her words rise like steam from the soup.

I nod. Mama knows what I've been up to. Politeness can be a cheap shield to protect your heart. And shields to protect hearts end up being prisons for hearts. But there are days I'd rather my heart be in a prison of my own making than be chopped liver in anyone else's hands.

"Look, Mama. Live like glass? Be transparent? And you can find yourself shattered." I find Mama's eyes. "Let people see past the surface, past your mask, even past your thoughts—and let people actually see your heart? An exposed heart can end up an executed heart. Having a glass heart—it can leave you cut."

And for a bowl of soup, my mama gives me my birthright. She says it slow—so I don't miss it, so I get back in touch with what matters, can be abundantly nourished by it. "Paying attention to hearts—is the only way to spend your life well." She reaches over and touches my hand. Her amputated finger lays on top of mine. The woman knows.

I have no idea if Mama had ever read about a nearly eighty-year-old-year study of the lives of Harvard students, but when her scarred and amputated finger rests there on the back of my hand, I can't help but think of the results of one of the world's longest longitudinal studies: "Close relationships, more than money or fame, are what keep people happy throughout their lives . . . Those ties protect people from life's discontents, help to delay mental and physical decline, and are better predictors of long and happy lives than social class, IQ, or even genes."[69]

Good relationships—are the crux of a good life.

Mama's tracing the back of my hand with her hand—with her one scarred and amputated finger.

Tying our hearts to other hearts turns out to be our best lifeline. The best stewardship of time is making time for relationship.

Even if it sometimes wounds.

"Loneliness kills," the director of this world-famous study had reported. "It's as powerful as smoking or alcoholism."

Mama, her hand stretched across the table, she's showing me how to reach out—and hold on. I can see it in her brave face, right there in her warm, wise eyes: the secret to healthy aging is healthy relationships, healthy relationships, healthy relationships. Old age can't keep you from love—but love can keep you from aging poorly.

I watch Mama ladle out more bowls of soup, set them around the table, watch how she lives given. She sets the last bowl down. And she lays it all down: "Live with walls to block out pain, and you will block out all the love that's trying to get in."

Light floods the kitchen, the table, and I claim my birthright: You have to let the love in. Open your arms wide open—and let the love in.

No one tells you that the walls you build to protect your heart end up being the walls that imprison your life. The walls you're building to keep the hurt out—they're the same walls that keep the healing from getting in.

Live with walls to block out pain, and you will block out all the love that's trying to get in.

What every broken heart needs is to break down its self-protecting walls. What every broken heart needs is to be vulnerable enough to share its brokenness. You will see as much healing in your life as you let people see the brokenness in your life. You are as healable as you are vulnerable.

I now look in the mirror and search that face with a question: Can you believe your heart is a gift? Your gift is not what you do, but who you are. And who He is in you. And He is making your heart into a gift.

Believe. Be brave and give your heart as a gift. You give what's good when you give what's in your hands—but you give what's eternal when you give what's in your heart. The only real gift you can give is a bit of your heart. The purpose of your life is to find your gift—and give it away.

What do you do with your one broken heart? You give it away. Give your heart to God in endless thanksgiving. And then give your broken heart to a hurting world in intentional acts of generosity, vulnerability, and transparency, so that you are healed with what always most heals a heart—intimacy.

Mama steps in and puts her arms around my shoulders, and she whispers it there at my ear, like an epiphany of light that could burn down all the walls: "Your job is not to find love. Your job is to find all the walls you've built to keep love out."

I reach out my hand to grab hers.

And this is always what happens. When you reach out and offer yourself like a gift, you break down the walls that are keeping the love out.

And in that moment I see what Mama has done with her life. What every woman has wanted for her life.

She's wanted to be brave. She's wanted to be the weakness of the best kind of strong. But most of all, she's wanted to become love. Abundant love. She's wanted to be a gift—to her people, to the world. She's wanted to reach out and be the gift and break down the walls that have kept love out. *All the abundant love.*

Because there's no better way any woman can live than to be the beauty of a gift. The good life lives given. Because Love is a verb and that verb is given and for God so loved the world—He gave. *Love lives given.*

Mama smiles.

And every reaching wrinkle for every smiling woman is a testament to her reaching out—and all the abundant love getting in.

- ✧ Quietly reflect on where you may have walls around your broken heart. Why have you built those walls? What would it look like to believe that your heart could be given as a gift?
- ✧ How might braving transparency let abundant love into your life? What would it look like to take the way of abundance?

Devotion 60

CRUCIFORMATION

"The love of most will grow cold, but the one who stands firm to the end will be saved."

MATTHEW 24:12–13

Now this is the thing it's taken me too long to realize: what you want is who you are. You are what your heart beats for, seeks for, reaches for. You are what your heart loves, desires, admires, acquires.

What your heart wants is who you are.

And I confess I've wanted safety, security, guarantees, wanted to stand with the comfort of the majority, make affirmation or validation my priority, or be about self-improvement primarily, be about stability and popularity and familiarity.

And it's taken me too much of my life to realize: what I really want is really my God. And do I really want an abundance of God?

Jesus isn't about just forming my mind; He's about forming my heart to want what He wants. To love what He loves, to walk the Via Dolorosa, to take the broken way of abundance that He takes, to form my broken heart into a self-giving, self-sacrificing, cruciform love like His abundant love.

Because what we love most is our most basic orientation, our baseline inclination, our default orientation that generates how we move forward, and we're all moving forward toward something and what is that something, *Someone*, that you really want?

What you really want is who you really are. And what you ultimately love is ultimately your identity. And how do you put on Christ?

How am I formed and shaped like Christ, formed and shaped like a cross—cruciform?

This is what took me too long to know: spiritual formation is ultimately cruciformation.

Cruciformation—it's an actual scientific definition, an actual term in biology referring to the transformation from lineform DNA to cruciform DNA, cross-shaped DNA. Draw a cross on your wrist every day and ask: What do I want? What do I love? And this cultural moment is begging the DNA of all things to transform from a linear worldview, from a flatline view of the world, to a cross-shaped view of everything.

From flat screens, from flat faith, from flatline living to cross-shaped thinking, cross-shaped seeing, cross-shaped choosing, cross-shaped living. The way a life genuinely transforms into abundance is to become genuinely cruciform.

We are the Jesus followers who are called to literally follow the One who looked us in the eye and said, "If I die, I die." So how can we live anything less? Now is the time, this generation, to be configured by our imitation of Christ, and now is the time to live cruciformation.

It can be easy to miss that nothing matters more than this. It can be easy to miss that there's a crisis of discipleship wherever we love the wrong things. That there's a crisis of worship wherever there's loving safety more than loving obeying the Savior, wherever we want to protect our lives more than lay down our own lives, where we love ladders to the good life more than dying to live the abundant life.

Wherever we love comfort more than the cross, wherever we want self-protection over dying to self, it can be easy to miss this crisis of worship in how we form our time, our choices. But how we form our days is forming us. Everything we do is forming us. Turning to Facebook forms where we turn our faces. Turning to screens forms our hearts. And if we want abundant transformation, Christ must be our orientation.

Are we formed by the world or the Word, by the news or the good news, by the culture or the cross?

It can be easy to miss that there's a crisis of discipleship wherever there's a crisis of fellowship, and a crisis of citizenship wherever there's more loyalty to self and to nation. It can be easy to miss that what you want is who you are. And you love what you are willing to die for. Are we willing to take the broken way of abundance and die in a thousand brave ways for the upside-down kingdom of Christ?

It can be easy to miss: our deepest security is found in deep cruciformity. No one ever got saved unless someone was willing to be unsafe. Why would we let fear overcome us when His arms are under us?

This is what I'm coming to know: there is a crisis of discipleship wherever there is a crisis of worship, of citizenship, of lordship and kingship. What would happen if the people who love the cross chose the Great Commission, not comfort—and became cross-centered, cross-shaped, abundantly cruciform?

You will become what you want most. Do you most want Jesus, the only One who has ever loved you to death and back *to the realest abundant life*?

Following Christ is more a matter of the reformation of the heart than about information for the head. What we really want is what we really worship . . . And there's a crisis of discipleship wherever we've forgotten our first love.

Sometimes I wonder: What makes us want to touch the screen of our phones when we could reach out and touch the heart of God? Do we most want the One whose love we have betrayed a thousand times but who never stops coming for us countless times? Do we love the One who comes and finds us when we're lost, who reminds us when we've forgotten who we are, who remakes us when life tries to break us?

Do you love the One who's bled His heart out for your broken heart, who's renamed you as His when everyone else rejected you as theirs? Who washed your grime and gave you grace, who took your place at the cross to give you the best place at the table? Who traced your bruises and touched your broken and whispered to your scars, *"You are my beloved"*?

The cross of Jesus proves He doesn't ultimately expect your perfection. The arms of Jesus on the cross prove He ultimately wants your affection. *Return to your first love.*

Jesus, the only One who ever loved us to death, He died with arms open wide, in cruciformation, as a saving, self-giving invitation. He died the way He abundantly lived—and now we can live as His imitation.

Dare to take the broken way of abundance and become cruciform. Live broken and given like bread. Because this broken way of abundance—this will transform the world.

FOR REFLECTION

- ✧ Look back at this journey into the way of abundance. What has God revealed to you about Himself? About yourself? What brokenness in your life is preventing you from wanting what God wants, loving what He loves—preventing you from wanting an abundance of God?
- ✧ As you have moved into this way of abundance, of living a deeply meaningful life, how has God moved you? How has living broken and given and loved, cruciform, into the abundant life, been an unexpected and fulfilling way to genuinely transform? What are other ways you can commit to the abundant way of cruciformation to continue the transformation of your soul and the world?

Acknowledgments

Sometimes you just long to singularly acknowledge one person, long to acknowledge where you've come from. Long to acknowledge who has walked the way before you since the beginning, your beginning—shown you more of the abundant way with bits of their brave lives, brave hearts.

Mama, you have been the bravest—and your brave has won ten thousand battles because it's made us all braver countless times. We have all watched you boldly take the way of abundance, no matter how the road seemed to wind through broken valleys that turned into the valley of His cupped hands.

We have watched you take the way of abundance, no matter how the way twisted through wildernesses where He wooed, where He never brings us to abandon us, but to always bring us closer.

We have watched you take the way of abundance, no matter how it seemed like it didn't matter—because God makes meaning out of our messes, because He is the God who can make all our brokenness into abundance, because you and I say this back to each other over and over again: *The Writer of the story has written Himself into the hardest places of yours and is softening the broken edges of everything with redeeming, abundant grace.*

So, like you always tell me, Mama, *all is always well, in every way. Abundantly well.*

NOTES

1. Victor Hugo, *Les Misérables*, vol. 1 in *The Works of Victor Hugo* (Boston: Little, Brown, 1887), 328.
2. Matthew 27:46.
3. Matthew 9:12.
4. John 9:3 MSG.
5. John 9:3 NLT.
6. Isaiah 61:1.
7. Charles H. Spurgeon, "Christ's Hospital: A Sermon on Psalm 147:3," Metropolitan Tabernacle Pulpit, http://archive.spurgeon.org/sermons/2260.php.
8. Quoted in Vanessa Thorpe, "Magical Realism . . . and Fakery," *Guardian online* (January 21, 2001), www.theguardian.com/world/2001/jan/21/books.booksnews.
9. 1 Corinthians 1:9, my paraphrase.
10. Matthew 16:25.
11. See Julietta Jameson, *Cliffy: The Cliff Young Story* (Melbourne, Australia: Text Publishing, 2013).
12. Martin Luther King Jr., *A Gift of Love: Sermons from* Strength to Love *and Other Preachings* (Boston: Beacon, 1963), 49.
13. 1 Corinthians 13:8 MSG.
14. Simone Weil, from an April 13, 1942, letter to poet Joë Bousquet, published in their collected correspondence (*Correspondance* [Lausanne: Editions l'Age d'Homme, 1982], 18).
15. Saint Ignatius, in a letter to Ascanio Colonna (Rome, April 25, 1543),

quoted in "Abandoning Ourselves to His Hands," Bishop Felipe J. Estévez, *St. Augustine Catholic* (September/October 2014), 7, http://faithdigital.org/staugustine/SA0914/03197846597C1F18B6D8F09EB9D106CC/SA1014.pdf.

16. John 3:16, emphasis added.
17. C. S. Lewis, *Mere Christianity* (1943; repr., New York: Macmillan, 1960), 153, 170.
18. Dietrich Bonhoeffer, *The Cost of Discipleship* (1949; repr., New York: Macmillan, 1963), 99.
19. Lewis, *Mere Christianity*, 167.
20. Lewis, *Mere Christianity*, 167.
21. Lewis, *Mere Christianity*, 167.
22. Lewis, *Mere Christianity*, 167–68.
23. Quoted in Jack Wellman, "Oswald Chambers: Biography, Quotes and Role in Christian History," *Patheos* (May 25, 2014), www.patheos.com/blogs/christiancrier/2014/05/25/oswald-chambers-biography-quotes-and-role-in-christian-history.
24. James Aughey, quoted in Charles Noel Douglas, ed., *Forty Thousand Sublime and Beautiful Thoughts* (New York: Christian Herald, 1915), 957.
25. Mark 8:34 MSG.
26. C. S. Lewis, *Till We Have Faces: A Myth Retold* (New York: Harcourt, Brace, 1956), 111.
27. Romans 5:8.
28. 1 Corinthians 13:7 ESV.
29. Brother Lawrence, *The Practice of the Presence of God* (London: Allenson, 1906), 26.
30. John 9:3, my paraphrase.
31. Luke 19:9.
32. Luke 19:6 ESV.
33. Quoted in Charles J. Healy, *Praying with the Jesuits: Finding God in All Things* (Mahwah, NJ: Paulist, 2011), 45.
34. Genesis 37–50.
35. Numbers 16.
36. Mark 8:4 CSB.

37. 2 Corinthians 8:9.
38. Eugene Peterson, "Introduction to the Books of Moses," in *The Message: The Bible in Contemporary Language* (Colorado Springs: NavPress, 2002), 17.
39. Nicholas Wolterstorff, *Lament for a Son* (Grand Rapids: Eerdmans, 1987), 84.
40. Romans 12:13 ESV.
41. Luke 22:19.
42. Martin Luther King Jr., "The American Dream," sermon at Ebenezer Baptist Church, Atlanta, Georgia (July 4, 1965), http://king encyclopedia.stanford.edu/encyclopedia/documentsentry/doc_the_american_dream.1.html.
43. Martin Luther King Jr., *Strength to Love* (New York: Harper & Row, 1963), 72.
44. Leviticus 19:34.
45. Job 31:32.
46. Ruth 2:10 MSG.
47. Shūsaku Endō, *Silence: A Novel* (1969; repr., New York: Picador, 2016), 92.
48. Matthew 25:44.
49. Matthew 5:43 MSG.
50. Martin Luther, "The 95 Theses," www.reformed.org/documents/95_theses.html.
51. Mark 1:15.
52. See Max Lucado, "Woodcutter's Wisdom and Other Favorite Stories" (March 22, 2012), https://maxlucado.com/woodcutters-wisdom-and-other-favorite-stories.
53. Lewis, *Mere Christianity*, 165.
54. Romans 7:24.
55. C. S. Lewis, *Letters to Malcolm: Chiefly on Prayer* (New York: Harcourt, Brace & World, 1964), 91.
56. Luke 19:41–42.
57. Based on Prayer LXXV in Bishop Nikolai Velimirović, *Prayers by the Lake* (Grayslake, IL: Serbian Orthodox Metropolitanate of New Gracanica, 1999), www.sv-luka.org/praylake/pl75.htm.

58. 2 Corinthians 1:3–4 ESV.

59. Amos 8:11–12.

60. Rod Dreher, "The Cost of 'Narrative Collapse,'" *American Conservative* (February 17, 2014), www.theamericanconservative.com/dreher/the-cost-of-narrative-collapse.

61. Luke 24:15–16, 27, 30–32.

62. Matthew 5:44.

63. Psalm 90:12, my paraphrase.

64. Charles Haddon Spurgeon, *Spurgeon's Sermons on Great Prayers of the Bible* (Grand Rapids: Kregel, 1995), 31.

65. Elisabeth Elliot, quoted in *Gateway to Joy*, "The Furnace of Affliction," Back to the Bible, http://web.archive.org/web/20140818143351/http://www.backtothebible.org:80/index.php/Gateway-to-Joy/Defining-Suffering.html.

66. 2 Kings 5:11–12.

67. Timothy Keller, *Generous Justice: How God's Grace Makes Us Just* (New York: Dutton, 2012), 177.

68. Keller, *Generous Justice*, 177, 180.

69. Liz Mineo, "Good Genes Are Nice, but Joy Is Better," *Harvard Gazette* (April 11, 2017), https://news.harvard.edu/gazette/story/2017/04/over-nearly-80-years-harvard-study-has-been-showing-how-to-live-a-healthy-and-happy-life.

The Broken Way

A Daring Path into the Abundant Life

Ann Voskamp

There's a way that beckons you into more time, more meaning, more authentic relationships. There's a way, especially when things aren't shaping up quite like you imagined, that makes life take the shape of more—more abundance, more intimacy, more God.

New York Times bestselling author Ann Voskamp asks the questions not one of us can afford to ignore:

- What do you do with your unspoken broken?
- What's the answer to suffering, to the brokenness of all our hearts?
- What do you do if you really want to know abundant wholeness—before it's too late?

There's a way of honest, transformative power.
Dare to take the broken way—to abundance.

Available in stores and online!

The Broken Way Study Guide with DVD

Ann Voskamp

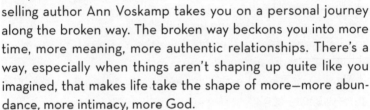

In this six-session video Bible study, New York Times best-selling author Ann Voskamp takes you on a personal journey along the broken way. The broken way beckons you into more time, more meaning, more authentic relationships. There's a way, especially when things aren't shaping up quite like you imagined, that makes life take the shape of more—more abundance, more intimacy, more God.

Sessions include:

- How Do We Live This One Broken Life?
- Living Cruciform
- Learning to Receive
- Real *Koinonia*
- Embracing Inconvenience
- Who We Serve

Dare to take the broken way—to abundance.

One Thousand Gifts

A Dare to Live Fully Right Where You Are

Ann Voskamp

Like most readers, Ann Voskamp hungers to live her one life well. Forget the bucket lists about once-in-a-lifetime experiences.

"How," Ann wondered, "do we find joy in the midst of deadlines, debt, drama, and daily duties? What does a life of gratitude look like when your days are gritty, long, and sometimes dark? What is God providing here and now?

A beautifully practical guide to living a life of joy, *One Thousand Gifts* invites you to wake up to God's everyday blessings. As Voskamp discovered, in giving thanks for the life she already had, she found the life she'd always wanted.

Following Voskamp's grace-bathed reflections on her farming, parenting, and writing life, you will embark on the transformative spiritual discipline of chronicling gifts. You will discover a way of seeing that opens your eyes to gratitude, a way of living so you are not afraid to die, and a way of becoming present to God's presence that brings deep and lasting happiness.

Also available:

One Thousand Gifts in both blue and brown duotone
   leather editions
One Thousand Gifts Study Guide with DVD
*One Thousand Gifts Devotional: Reflections on Finding
   Everyday Grace*
*Selections from One Thousand Gifts: Finding Joy
   in What Really Matters*